ORDINARY TIME

T012II53

ORDI-NARY TIME

Cycles in Marriage, Faith, and Renewal

Nancy Mairs

BEACON PRESS   BOSTON

Beacon Press
25 Beacon Street
Boston, Massachusetts 02108-2892

Beacon Press books
are published under the auspices of
the Unitarian Universalist Association of Congregations.

An earlier version of "Here: Grace" appeared in
Books and Religion 18, no. 2 (Summer 1991). Excerpt from "Singapore,"
from *House of Light* by Mary Oliver, copyright © 1990 by Mary
Oliver, reprinted by permission of Beacon Press.

This book was supported in part by a fellowship from the National
Endowment for the Arts.

Text design by Copenhaver Cumpston

Library of Congress Cataloging-in-Publication Data

Mairs, Nancy, 1943–
Ordinary time: cycles in marriage, faith, and renewal /
Nancy Mairs.
p.   cm.
Includes bibliographical references.
ISBN 0-8070-7056-4 (cloth)
ISBN 0-8070-7057-2 (paper)
1. Spiritual life—Catholic authors.   2. Mairs, Nancy, 1943–
3. Women in the Catholic Church—United
States.   4. Feminism—
Religious aspects—Catholic Church.   I. Title.
BX2350.2.M3144   1993
248.4'82—dc20   92-40421
CIP

For George
with whom I have spent all my best times
ordinary and otherwise

If the world were only pain and logic, who would want it?

—Mary Oliver, "Singapore"

CONTENTS

ACKNOWLEDGMENTS

"It occurs to me that perhaps you might write about the development and enactment of a social conscience," my editor for *Remembering the Bone House*, Lisa Miles, wrote as we were readying the manuscript for publication, since "I didn't really let you express that aspect of yourself in this book." I had no idea of the terrors and complexities her suggestion would lead to as I worked my way through the terrain of a conscientious life, but I am grateful to her nevertheless for sensing that *Bone House*, with its emphasis on bodily experience, asked for a spiritual companion.

I am also grateful to my agent, Barbara S. Kouts, and to the people at Beacon Press for sharing that sense. My editor at Beacon, Andrew Hrycyna, provided the kind of attentive and exacting readings that renewed my resolve time and again. Others, too, read the manuscript in whole or in part, and my thanks go to them for their warm support: Susan Hardy Aiken, Ricardo Elford, Marie Harris, Eleanor Nudd, Karen Oakes, Jean Pedrick, and Barrie Ryan.

I learned that Beacon had accepted the proposal for *Ordinary Time* just as my husband and I were setting out for the hospital, where he would have a large malignant tumor removed from his small intestine. In the next few weeks, when it seemed likely that George would depart quite soon, I recognized in panic that I probably couldn't write any book, and certainly not this book, unless he read each essay as I finished it. Since I was seventeen, he has served as my primary reader, the one I must address before I can speak to the world beyond. Miraculously, I haven't had to put that superstition to the test. He has stayed for all of *Ordinary Time*, and next spring I hope to put a published copy in his hands, with my greatest gratitude.

Nancy Mairs
Tucson, Summer 1992

ORDINARY TIME

INTROIT: A WANTON GOSPELLER

I have spent the whole of my conscious life—against all principles of reason—in an uneasy and unrelenting state of religious faith, and as I hurtle toward the half-century mark, I find myself wanting with increasing urgency to know why and how I've done such a thing and what the consequences have been. The only way I can find out is through language, learning line by line as the words compose me. Other people may have developed different and more efficient strategies, but in order to know anything at all, I have to write a book.

"A memoir of my life as a female body," I used to say as

I wrote *Remembering the Bone House*, the book I now think of as the companion to this one. A writer needs such a descriptive tag, no matter how inelegant or incomplete, to satisfy the polite inquiries of people who clearly don't have an extra six or eight hours to hear about a project in the detail the writer's obsession insists it deserves. "A book of essays on being a Catholic feminist," I tell people who ask what I'm working on now. "You should excuse the oxymoron." Although similarly inexact, suggesting that Catholicism and feminism are my subjects rather than the lenses through which I scrutinize all the world, this reply is invariably good for a laugh, and it anticipates and deflects other responses I'd have a hard time dealing with: gasps of incredulity, cringes of embarrassment, hoots of derision. It suggests that I'm smart enough to recognize without assistance the spiritual/social/intellectual dilemma I've skewered myself on. I may be foolhardy, it permits me to shrug wryly, but I'm not an utter fool.

My reply may be good for a laugh but, like many risible statements, it's not entirely facetious. Of all the not-notably-woman-friendly forms of Christianity, I have chosen—converted to—the most radically and intransigently misogynistic. Catholicism and feminism may really be, as philosophers like Mary Daly have concluded, incongruous beyond reconciliation, so that I can only bumble about in a spiritually astigmatic blur. And although not limited to the intersections of Catholicism with feminism, this book, like my life, takes much of its shape and significance from the ways in which I embody them both.

I've been at this Catholic feminist business for over a decade, and it hasn't gotten discernibly easier. Maybe, in some ways, harder. In fact, its very difficulty may be what pulls me along, I realized a couple of years ago. I'd been invited by the local Unitarian Universalist church to read from my work, and when I donated the meager profits from the evening to the church administrator, she thanked me for my generosity. "But it's really nothing," I laughed. "I *like* the Unitarians. I could easily *be* a Unitarian." Afterward, for some reason, that statement continued to resonate in my inner ear. It's true: I *could* easily be a Unitarian, with admirably lucid, sensible, liberal views to lead me firmly to right action in the world. And in that case, I could also more easily be a feminist, at least the kind of feminist I want to be (lucid, sensible, and radical).

I know plenty of lucid, sensible, right-acting, liberal or even radical—and feminist—Catholics, so obviously I haven't chosen an outright impossibility. But you'll have to admit that there's something murky and numinous right at the heart of the Christian mythos, especially in the emphasis on incarnation given it by Roman Catholicism, which no amount of reason can get around: a God who put on a body and walked about in that body and spoke to us from that body and died as that body and yet somehow did not die then or ever but lives on in our bodies which live in God. It's not the easiest story in the world to swallow. Then, to make matters worse, early on the story got into the wrong hands, the hands of some very anxiety-ridden and power-greedy men, many of whose fingers, white-knuckled, still contort and crush it, and in this mangled condition it has been used to kill millions of women and to cripple and confine countless more.

A Catholic feminist? Dear God, couldn't I please be something else?

If not, couldn't I at least keep a decent silence about my condition and work on some other book? I've started a novel about a woman who finds a skeleton walled up behind some shelves of old fruit preserves in her cellar. I'd like to get on with that. But this is the book that demands, by its refusal to drift into the region just beyond my sphere of attention where a growing host of book-shades have gathered, to be written. Someone more devout might see its tenacity as evidence of God's will, and maybe it is. Leery of human projections of personal desire onto God's inscrutable will, I rather suspect my own willfulness.

I was raised, in classical ladylike fashion, never to discuss religion, politics, or sex, and I'm still more comfortable with the weather than any other topic of conversation. When someone asks me with born-again fervor whether I've accepted Jesus Christ as my personal savior, I cringe; the question seems so intimate as to be slightly indecent. Religious belief is something like masturbation: You may do it—and it won't even make you crazy or give you warts if you do—but it's the sort of thing you keep to yourself.

Moreover, I have spent most of my career, and all my academic career, among secular humanists for whom *God* is a marker in a literary text, in the same way that *whale* is, or *Friday*, or *a room of one's own*. These are not things in which one believes. They may be objects of analysis, of interpretation, of appreciation, but certainly not of faith. Belief in a holy being would strike the people I'm thinking of as naive, even primitive, and public profession of it as therefore at least faintly embarrassing. And I share that embarrassment. So heavily have I bought into the intellectual establishment that I dread being judged simpleminded, even though simplicity of mind is, in several senses, precisely the quality I seek.

I feel another kind of embarrassment, even more daunting, in undertaking to write a book for which I lack credentials. The desire for expertise and the power of proof tempts me more deeply than anything else, because my whole life has trained me to feel it. To consult all the sources. To stack and sort the index cards. To arrive at the correct understanding of every term I use, every point I interpret. The thought of error makes me feel genuinely ill, queasy and feverish and unable to swallow. Since my doctoral work, though unorthodox, emphasized feminist theory, I feel entitled to a claim in this academic territory, the price per acre of which hasn't exactly gone through the ceiling anyway, though from the snarling and pissing on boundaries of some of the early occupants, you'd think the place was more precious than heaven. But the figures of theologians and biblical scholars loom like Cerberus at the doctrinal gates. *What right has she,* they ask one another, *to speak of matters about which she understands so little, and to get them so wrong? Religious truths are subtle, hard to get at, and enlightenment requires years of study and prayer and possibly even the hand of the Lord upon one's brow. It tends not to come to women at all, and certainly not to a woman who always leaves out one, though not always the same one, when enumerating the Seven Deadly Sins.*

Even feminist theologians like Mary Daly, Rosemary Radford Ruether, Carol Christ, and Elisabeth Schüssler Fiorenza, who have braved such patronizing sneers to open new spaces among the old boys, write with an authority that I have gone to some lengths to repudiate: I am a writer, not an author. They know what they're talking about, and I do not know what I'm talking about, not in the same sense. That is, they have achieved a certain mastery over their subject matter which they can assume their audience lacks but desires, and so they write with the confidence of experts. Instead of this authority, which establishes a distance from both self and other, I've chosen exploration and its attendant risks. It's as though some writers have the sense never to enter a room until they've thrown the switch and flooded it with light, whereas others, like me, insist on entering rooms with burnt-out bulbs or blown fuses or maybe no wiring at all.

I remember how eagerly I took up Ruether's *Disputed Questions*, described on the cover as a "personal odyssey of faith," and how let down I felt by its conventional, almost generic tone: The Spiritual Autobiography. The personal may be political, as the feminists say, but it doesn't seem to be religious. The questions in dispute ask themselves under the most general circumstances ("at college," "in the first ten years of marriage") and in the most general terms ("the meaning of Christian identity today"). Religious statements can be "existential, rather than merely propositional," Ruether says she discovered while a student at Scripps,[1] but she conveys only the most tenuous sense of her own or anyone else's existence.

Because I value Ruether's capacity for radical theological revision so highly, I can dismiss my disappointment in this one book readily enough. But my own work must come at the issues differently. The premises of my life have left me no choice. At the time I signed the contract to write *Ordinary Time*, my attention was given over to the exigencies of my husband's chemotherapy. "If God is going to be present to me," I recall reflecting one evening as George hunched in spasms over the pink plastic basin that accompanied us home from the hospital and remained within easy retrieving distance for months—never farther away than the linen closet even at the best of times—while I whispered encouragement and wiped sour strands from his lips and tears from his eyes, "she'll simply have to wade through the mess chemotherapy is currently making in our lives. I can't scramble away from it up to some loftier plain." Mine is, perforce, a practical expertise.

More intensely than I dread being taken for a fool, I fear that people will misread *Ordinary Time* as a textbook (if they are of an academic bent) or a sort of metaphysical Baedeker (if they have New Age leanings). They may read it as a prescription for carrying out the "righteous" life instead of as a search into the ways one woman deals with God's presence day after day. I'm not shirking some responsibility for telling people how best to live. I'm wholly unfitted for such a task. *I don't know.* And I don't want to appear to know. I don't want to be taken for some spiritual Julia Child, cooking up a main course of faith judiciously balanced by good works, with grace for a garnish, and salvation for a sweet: just follow my (incredibly complicated) instructions, dear readers, and you'll have a banquet fit for Saint Peter himself. Uh-uh. I want to find out how I ought best to live. It's the process of finding out that interests me. Moral inquiry, if you will, not moral preachments.

What *Ordinary Time* is not, then: a theological treatise; a formal exegesis of biblical or patristic texts; a systematic study of, or an apologetics for, Catholicism or feminism or any other "ism"; an exhortation to the ungodly to repent themselves of their sins and accept Jesus Christ as their personal savior; a self-help manual for inner children or wild men or women who love too much; a cookbook for conversion. Instead, I think of it as a kind of twentieth-century version of the spiritual autobiographies undertaken by my Puritan foremothers, which aims, as Mary G. Mason writes of Anne Bradstreet's brief "To My Dear Children," at a "harmonizing of the divine, the secular, and the personal, a unifying of a public and a private consciousness" by moving "from the inner circle of . . . husband, family, and community to the outward circle of God's providential creation."[2]

Although I am Anne Bradstreet's cultural (and, for all I know, her genealogical) daughter, she was more circumscribed by her communities than I am by mine. I needn't fear the kind of public chastisement meted out to my Puritan forebears which Nathaniel Hawthorne describes:

Side by side, on the meetinghouse steps, stood a male and a female figure. The man was a tall, lean, haggard personification of fanaticism, bearing on his breast this label,—A WANTON GOSPELLER,—which betokened that he had dared to give interpretations of Holy Writ, unsanctioned by the infallible judgment of the civil and religious rulers. His aspect showed no lack of zeal to maintain his heterodoxies, even at the stake. The woman wore a cleft stick on her tongue, in appropriate retribution for having wagged that unruly member against the elders of the church; and her countenance and gestures gave much cause to apprehend, that, the moment the stick should be removed, a repetition of the offence would demand new ingenuity in chastising it.[3]

My words are sanctioned by no one, and my tongue wags as it will, but since nowadays a wanton gospeller is likelier to be ignored than to be burnt at the stake, I can work pretty much on my own terms.

In hazarding public speech, I feel no drive toward proselytism. To be blunt, I have too much trouble bringing about my own conversions and commitments, day after day after day, to undertake anybody else's, and I have no intention of trying to persuade others to adopt precepts and ways of being with which I'm still struggling myself. Moreover, the endless replication of a single system for structuring beliefs and behaviors in relation to the whole complicated world outside one's skin strikes me as a dangerous idea. We're all human, after all, and in deciphering life's ambiguities, each of us is bound to get at least one point wrong. Safer to recognize our fallibility, generate a number of different imaginative patterns, and share them freely.

Choose God, if you like. Or Allah. Or Mother Earth. Or the double helix. Or chaos (I'm attracted to this one myself, since, from the human perspective, God certainly looks like a messy and absentminded housekeeper who never puts anything back in quite the same place twice). Since some systems lead to more life-enhancing ends than others do, I'd avoid capitalism if I were you. Communism appears to have removed itself from the running, but democratic socialism has not. Prefer, above all, a paradigm that tolerates and even encourages diversity. Any model (including the Catholic Church as it has functioned formally throughout most of its history) which discourages invention and forbids deviance from itself, especially on pain of death, will only sink us more deeply into the morass of bigotry we're already submerged in up to our bottom lips. If we don't want to go down with a glug, we'll have to imagine ourselves and our relationships in some other order altogether. We must stop projecting God outward as an overarching power—a kind of Strategic Defense Initiative, sacred or secular depending on your persuasion, with the capacity to blast the baddies (who are never ourselves, such a God being always on Our Side) into oblivion—and acknowledge personal responsibility for the God we choose and the ways in which we permit her into our lives.[4]

Ordinary Time represents one approach to relativizing God in this way. During the course of George's chemotherapy, I remember, I decided to buy a new refrigerator, and not until the day after I'd plunked down my five hundred dollars and arranged a date for delivery did it hit me that we might well not be around to get much use from that expense, considerable to people of our means. "Stupid, stupid," I chided myself. "One just gets into the habit of believing in one's future. One forgets about dying!" *Live as though you don't have cancer,* a voice in George's head had told him a couple of nights earlier. Sound advice, I thought. But did it extend to squandering money on a refrigerator? On the other hand, five hundred dollars wouldn't buy even one chemotherapy treatment, and if a new refrigerator would make our lives—whatever their length—easier, wasn't the money well spent? I was sick of such questions. I wished I were living a life that didn't necessitate them. Their very mundanity is what I've struggled with in conceiving *Ordinary Time*, though. Refrigerators and the wisdom or folly of their purchase do not belong in books about religious belief and religious practice, convention tells me. Refrigerators are profane: before the temple, not within its sacred precincts. God does not concern himself with appliances.

This kind of split makes me crazy, this territorializing of the holy. Here God may dwell. Here God may not dwell. It contradicts everything in my experience, which says: God dwells where I dwell. Period. I could give a clearer sense of this homeliness of the holy, I know, if I could make my mind up what I mean by "God." Instead, I have to make God up, over and over again, adding fresh layers of comprehension, responding with new capacities for belief, in the protracted process I've come to know as conversion. God begins, I once wrote to my friend Richard only half facetiously, as a kind of back formation: "The protectiveness and fear" he had expressed for his newborn son "ring so true, and they go on forever (or at least as far into forever as I've gotten). Parenthood teaches—forces?—prayer: Please God don't let him stop breathing in his crib, you say now, and in no time at all he'll be off in Zimbabwe and you'll be saying, Don't let him get cerebral malaria or fall off his moto and need a transfusion of AIDS-contaminated blood or fail to see in time the next cobra that shows up in his kitchen. We don't pray because God requires our petitions; we invent God so as to have some excuse for all those incoherent mumblings."

This is true to my experience: I have prayed, generally in this petitionary style in response to some aboriginal terror, for as long as I can remember. But it falls far short of my whole experience. How, I wonder, do people who don't believe in God account for life's mysteries and marvels? For the sense I recall, while sitting alone-in Chaco Canyon on a hot August afternoon, of an extra presence: not my self, or the ruined pueblo at my back, or the scrubby vegetation, or the hawk wheeling above the canyon floor and the rodent who must be scuttling from bush to bush to make the hawk's vigil worthwhile, but Something Else? That presence has also been with me as long as I can remember, so that I have never felt wholly alone, although I've often enough been lonely for human company. (I've never dared ask others whether they feel accompanied in this enigmatic way, though I could ask George. His is the presence I'll one day be loneliest for: the one of whom I can ask such a question.)

My motivation in writing *Ordinary Time* has been to examine this singular absolute of my existence: God is here. And here, and here, and here. Not an immutable entity detached from time but a continual calling and coming into being. Not transcendence, that orgy of self-alienation beloved of the fathers, but immanence: God working out Godself in every thing. Process, yes, that's what I want to explore and celebrate, the holy as verb, Godding, not Godness or Godhood. What she does. How she does it. One can't be an expert in process. By its very nature process can't be mastered. Because it's not finished. And who knows what will happen next? Does God herself? I doubt it. Not in the human sense of "know," which always implies control, possession, grasp: nothing slippery, nothing surprising. I'm certain that God slips and surprises more gloriously than Gerard Manley Hopkins's stippled trout.

I can't prove it, though. Proof is a function of language, and language, even at its most anagogical, is essentially rigorous. Whenever one speaks *God*, God goes stiff as a corpse. One of my favorite cartoons shows two mathematicians in front of a chalkboard on which is written an elaborate equation, the second term of which reads "then a miracle occurs." "I think," says one mathematician to the other, "you need to be more explicit here, in step two." God dwells in step two. Precise terms, no matter how intricate, will never quite catch God in the act. Just as a wave, at the instant of observation, collapses into a particle, at the moment of utterance the potentiality of God coalesces and freezes into Something That She Is but not All That She Is. As a writer, a wordsmith, I have taken on the one task I can be certain never to carry all the way out.

Such a project can only be exploratory and descriptive, not precise and prescriptive, and it must be rooted in experience, not just at its origin but throughout, all the way, as far as anyone can go (and we all know into what that always is). Otherwise, it degenerates into scholasticism or casuistry or pietism, all in their own ways designed to obscure or deny the contexts through which the holy erupts into humanity: the death of a father, the love of a good man, pregnancy, adultery, crippled limbs, soup kitchens, pink basins. . . . My exploration begins "here," with an essay that sketches the spiritual terrain I occupy now. Thereafter, four roughly chronological essays trace my "progress" from my Congregationalist childhood to my current status, however provisional, as a practicing Roman Catholic. The essays in parts 2 and 3 are written from this ground, "Daily Bread" focusing on the intimate relations that arise from marriage and motherhood and "Now and Forever" looking outward into the world and beyond.

Throughout, in order to avoid the temptation to withdraw into abstractions, whether intellectual, moral, or spiritual, I have kept my questions practical: What does it mean to live a life in God's presence? Present to God? What responsibilities do I bear in creating such a life? What choices must I make in order to sustain it? A book of personal essays written from the viewpoint of a Catholic feminist isn't going to get either you or me into heaven or, for that matter, into hell. Nothing here will lift us out of this world; on the contrary, I hope that you will plunge, as I have done, ever deeper into earthly existence, where we are needed. This is just life I'm writing about, after all, and life outside the seasons of fast and feast—Advent and Christmas, Lent and Easter—at that: ordinary time.

PART ONE

Getting Here
from There

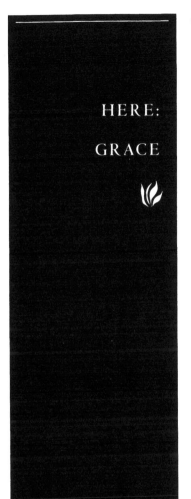

HERE:
GRACE

Y ou will love me?" my husband asks, and at something in his tone my consciousness rouses like a startled cat, ears pricked, pupils round and onyx-black.

Never voluble, he has been unusually subdued this evening. Thinking him depressed about the mysterious symptoms that have plagued him for months and that we know in our heart of hearts signal a recurrence of cancer, although the tests won't confirm it for several more days, I pressed up against him on the couch and whispered against his neck, "This may be the most troublesome time of our lives, but I'm so happy." This awareness of joy, though it's been growing for several years now, has recently expanded in response to my own failing health. A few weeks ago, pondering the possibility that I might die at any time, I posed myself a new question: *If I died at this very moment, would I die happy?* And the answer burst out without hesitation: *Yes!* Since then, in spite of my fears, I've felt a new contentment. What more could I ever ask than to give an unequivocal response to such a question?

His silence persisted. "Scared?" I asked him after a few moments, thinking of the doctor's appointment that morning, the CAT scan scheduled for later in the week. Head resting on the back of the couch, eyes closed, he nodded. More silence. Finally I said, "George, you know how I love words. I need words!"

And now, words: "You will love me?" Behind his glasses, his eyes have the startled look I associate, incongruously, with the moment of orgasm.

"Yes," I tell him, alert, icy all over. "I can safely promise you that. I will always love you."

"You asked the other day whether my illness could be AIDS," he says unevenly. "I'm pretty sure it isn't, because I had the test for HIV some time ago, after I had an affair for a couple of years with another woman."

The sensation is absolutely nonverbal, but everybody knows it even without words: the stunned breathlessness that follows a jab to the solar plexus. What will astonish me in the days to come is that this sensation can sustain itself long after one would expect to be dead of asphyxiation. I have often wished myself dead. If it were possible to die of grief, I would die at this moment. But it's not, and I don't.

A couple of years. *A couple of years.* This was no fit of passion, no passing fancy, but a sustained commitment. He loved her, loves her still: Their relationship, until he broke it off—for reasons having little to do with me—was a kind of marriage, he says. Time after time after time he went to her, deliberately, telling whatever lies he needed to free himself from me and the children, and later from his mother when she came for a protracted visit after his father's death, throughout at least a couple of years.

More. He'd fallen in love with her six years earlier, I could sense at that time, and they'd had a prolonged flirtation. She was a bitter, brittle woman, and something about her rage inflamed him. Their paths had parted, however, and I had no way of knowing of their later chance encounter, courtship, years-long "marriage." And after that ended—here, in this room, which will ever hereafter be haunted by her tears—four years of silence: too late to tell me, he says, and then too later, and then too later still. Twelve of our twenty-seven years of marriage suddenly called, one way or another, into question. I recall my brother's description of his framing shop after the San Francisco earthquake, how miraculously nothing in it was broken, not even the sheets of glass for covering pictures, but it looked as though some giant gremlin had come in and slid everything a few feet to one side. My past feels similarly shoved out of whack, not shattered but strangely reconfigured, and out of its shadows steps a man I have never seen before: Sandra's lover.

If I were that proverbial virtuous woman, the one whose price is far above rubies, perhaps I would have the right to order George out of my sight, out of my house, out of my life. But I'm not that woman. I'm the other one, the one whose accusers dropped their stones and skulked away. I've desired other men, slept with them, even loved them, although I've never felt married to one. I guess I took my girlhood vow literally: I have always thought of marriage as something one did once and for-ever. All the same, in brief passionate bursts I've transgressed the sexual taboos that give definition to Christian marriage.

I'm not a virtuous woman, but I am a candid one. Many years ago, George and I pledged that we would not again lie to anyone about anything. I haven't been strictly faithful to the spirit of this promise, either, because I've deliberately with-held information on occasion (although not, according to my mother, often enough, having an unfortunate propensity for spilling the family beans in print); but I have not, when directly challenged, lied. This commitment can have maddening con-sequences: One night I listened for half an hour or longer to the outpourings of a total stranger in response to an essay in one of my books because I couldn't tell her that I had a pot on the stove about to boil over when I actually didn't. Had Daddy and I meant that vow for *everybody*, my daughter asked after I hung up the telephone, not just for each other? Not even, I can see now, for each other: especially not for each other.

"How can you ever believe me again after this?" George asks, and I shrug: "I've believed you all this time. I'm in the habit of it. Why should I stop now?" And so I go on believing him, but a subtle difference will emerge over time: belief becomes a matter of faith, no longer logically connected to the "truth" of its object, which remains unknowable except insofar as it chooses to reveal itself. I suppose I could hire a private detective to corroborate George's tales, but I'm not going to because George's whereabouts are no less his own business now than they ever were. I can envision some practical difficulties in my being unable to locate him at any given time, but no moral ones, whereas I perceive a serious problem in seeking information that would curb his freedom to lie, a freedom without which he can't freely tell me the truth. I don't want to come by my belief through extortion. Once, I believed George because it never occurred to me not to believe him; now I believe him because I prefer belief, which affirms his goodness, to doubt, which sneers and sniggers at it. No longer an habitual response, belief becomes an act of love.

It does not thereby absolve George of responsibility for the choices he has freely made, however. The years while he was slipping away to sleep with Sandra were among the most wretched of my not conspicuously cheerful life; and by lying to me, he permitted—no, really encouraged—me to believe that my unhappiness was, as always, my own fault, even though, thanks to the wonders of psychopharmacology, I was at last no longer clinically depressed. I remember lying awake, night after night, while he stayed up late grading papers and then dropped into bed, and instantly into sleep, without a word or a touch; as he twitched and snored, I'd prowl through the dark house, sip milk or wine, smoke cigarettes, write in my journal until, shuddering with cold and loneliness, I'd be forced to creep back into bed. Past forty, he must have been conserving his sexual energies, I realize now, but when I expressed concern and sadness, he blamed our chilling relationship on me: I was distracted, too bitchy, not affectionate enough. . . . Ah, he knew my self-doubts thoroughly.

Breakdowns in our relationship, especially sexual ones, had habitually been ascribed to me. "I'm very tired," I wrote in my journal early in this period of misery, twenty years into our marriage, "of his putting me down all the time—telling me that I'm too involved with Anne, that I don't handle Matthew well, that I'm not affectionate (the only signs of affection he recognizes are physical, which I suppose makes sense, since he doesn't communicate verbally). In short, that I'm a bad mother and wife. I just don't know how to feel much affection for someone I feel sorry for, for being married to me." Tired of disparagement I may already have been, but I took over two years more to recognize myself as a collaborator in it: "He survives—thrives—on my culpability. Without it, where would he be today? We've *both* built our lives on it, and if I remove it, our relationship will no longer have any foundation."

This awareness of complicity precipitated out of a homely crisis (the form of most of my crises), in the winter of 1985, involving the proper setting of the thermostat, which George persistently left at sixty degrees even though I couldn't bear the temperature below sixty-five (and, as came out in the course of the dispute, neither could he). When I told him that the coldness of the house represented my growing feelings of neglect and abandonment, he countered that he had to go elsewhere (leaving the thermostat set at sixty) in order to get the touching and affection he needed. It was, I noted, "the same old ploy, trying to trigger my guilt for not being a physically affectionate wife. Only this time I could feel myself not quite biting. Because he wants the physical part to continue regardless of the pain I'm in, even if he causes the pain, and he blames me if I won't put out, come across, what have you. And I'm sick unto death of bearing the blame." He could, I suddenly understood, turn up the heat himself. He chose not to.

Or rather, he chose to turn it up in some other woman's house. In spite of the sexual stresses underlying this controversy, he gave no hint that his longing for "warmth and light" was taking him from the crumbling converted Chinese grocery where the children and I lived to a spacious, immaculate, perfectly appointed home in a tranquil neighborhood miles away; and I didn't guess. Just as he knew how to exploit my self-doubts, he knew how to escape me. Teaching in two programs, he was out of the house from at least eight-thirty in the morning until eight-thirty at night; he devoted his spare time to good works like cooking at Casa María soup kitchen, observing the federal trial of the people who had arranged sanctuary for refugees from El Salvador, and editing ¡Presente!, the local Catholics for Peace and Justice newsletter. With such a schedule, of course he'd have little enough energy left for sex, or even a leisurely family dinner. Another woman (his lover, for instance) might have judged his devotion to illiterate, poor, and oppressed people sanctimonious, even morbid, but I found it natural and necessary.

As a result, he put me in a conscientious bind: I felt abandoned, and I believed that George was neglecting our troubled teenaged son dangerously, but I couldn't make our needs weigh heavily enough against those of five hundred empty bellies at the kitchen door or a Salvadoran woman who'd fled her village in terror when the last of her sons disappeared. Still, I wondered uneasily why the spiritual growth he said he was seeking necessitated his setting out on what appeared to be "a quest—Galahad and the Holy Grail—noble and high-minded and above all out there, beyond the muck and mire of daily living in a decaying house with a crippled wife and a rebellious adolescent son." Forced to let him go, I did so with a bitter blessing: "Feed the poor, my dear. Shelter the refugees. Forget the impoverishment you leave in your wake. It's only Nancy and Matthew and Anne, after all—nothing spiritual there, nothing uplifting, no real needs, just niggling demands that drag at you, cling to you, slow your lofty ascent into the light and life of Christ."

Our approaches to ministry were hopelessly at odds: "I think that the life of Christ is only this life, which one must enter further and further. And I hate the entering. I'd give anything to escape. . . . There's no glamor here, no glory. Only the endless grading of papers. The being present for two difficult children. The making of another meal. The dragging around of an increasingly crippled body, forcing it to one end of the house and back again, out the door, into the classroom, home again, up from the bed, up from the toilet, up from the couch.

The extent of my lofty ascent. I want only to do what I must with as much grace as I can." That George, finding these conditions squalid and limiting, sought to minister elsewhere embittered but hardly surprised me. And so, whenever he wanted Sandra, he had only to murmur "Soup. Sanctuary. *¡Presente!*" in order to be as free of them as he liked.

I have been, it appears, a bit of a fool. "Where did I think you'd gone?" I ask George. "What lies did I believe?" He claims not to remember. He will always claim not to remember such details, which is his prerogative, but the writer in me obsessively scribbles in all the blanks he leaves. I imagine the two of them sitting half-naked beside her pool, sipping cold Coronas and laughing at my naïveté, and then I have to laugh myself: I would have been the last thing on their minds. This sense of my own extinction will prove the most tenacious and terrifying of my responses, the one that keeps me flat on my back in the night, staring into the dark, gasping for breath, as though I've been buried alive. For almost thirty years, except during a couple of severe disintegrative episodes, my presence to George has kept me present to myself. Now, at just the moment when cancer threatens to remove that reassurance of my own reality from my future, it's yanked from my past as well. Throughout his sweet stolen hours with Sandra, George lived where I was not.

"Are you all right?" my daughter asks on the day following George's revelation when she stumbles upon me huddled in my studio, rocking and shivering. I shake my head. "Shall I cut class and stay here with you?"

"No, go to class," I say. "Then come back. We'll talk."

"You're not going to do anything rash while I'm gone?" It's

the question of a child seasoned in suicide, and I wish she didn't have to ask it.

"I promise. Scoot."

I hadn't planned to tell Anne, at least not yet; but George is getting sicker by the day, his mother is about to arrive for several weeks, Christmas is coming, and I don't think I can deal with this new complication alone. I have George's permission to tell whomever I wish. "I want you to write about this," he says. "I want you to write about us." For himself, he has never revealed it to anyone except once, early on, the psychotherapist with whom we've worked, together and apart, over the years. But he believes in the value of what I try to do in my work: in reclaiming human experience, insofar as I can find it embodied in my own experience, from the morass of secrecy and shame into which Christian and pre-Christian social taboos have plunged it, to rescue and restore God's good creation. (And if at times the work proves as smelly as pumping a septic tank, well, shit is God's creation, too.) George supports it, but the work itself is mine. If any bad tidings are to be borne, I am the one to bear them.

"But Mom," Anne says when I've finished my tale of woe, "men *do* these things." Transcribed, these words might look like a twenty-five-year-old's cynicism, but in fact her tone rings purely, and characteristically, pragmatic. It's just the tone I need to jerk my attention back from private misery to the human condition. She's right, of course. In the Judaic roots of our culture, as Uta Ranke-Heinemann points out in *Eunuchs for the Kingdom of Heaven*, "a man could never violate his own marriage. The wife belonged to her husband, but the husband did not belong to his wife,"[1] and a couple of thousand years of Church teaching on the subject of marital fidelity—not all of it a model of clarity and consistency—has never entirely balanced the expectations placed on the two partners. *People* do these things, Anne means (I know: I have done them myself); but ordinary men, men possessed of healthy sexual appetites, have been tacitly *entitled* to do them. They're just *like* that.

Except for my man. One reviewer of my first book of essays, *Plaintext*, wrote: "The reader will also wish to see more closely some of the people who simply drift through these essays, especially Mairs' husband, who comes across as a saint, staying through extreme mood swings, suicide attempts, severe illness, and a number of love affairs." That's *my* man: a saint. Through my essays I've publicly canonized him. Any man who could stay with a crazy, crippled, unfaithful bitch like me had to be more than humanly patient and loving and long-suffering and self-abnegating and . . . oh, just more than human.

Admittedly, I had help in forming this view, especially from other women; a man whose bearing is as gentle and courtly as George's can seem a true miracle, one my inconstancy plainly didn't merit. "But hasn't he ever slept with another woman?" more than one person has asked, and I've said proudly, gratefully, "No. I've asked him, and he tells me he never has." I often told myself that he "ought to go, get out now, while he's still fairly young, find a healthy woman free from black spells, have some fun. No one could blame him." And occasionally, trying to account for his physical and emotional unavailability, I'd conjecture: "Perhaps another woman—he's so attractive and romantic that that thought always crosses my mind." My guess was dead on, it turns out, formed at the height of his affair with just the sort of healthy woman I'd had in mind, but I took him at his word and felt humbled—humiliated—that he had responded to my infidelities with such steadfastness.

A saint's wife readily falls prey to self-loathing, I discovered, since comparisons are both common and invidious, and recuperation, if it occurs at all, is a protracted and lonely process.

One evening a couple of years ago, when I'd been invited to discuss *Plaintext* with a local women's reading group and the conversation turned, as such conversations always seem to, to my infidelity and George's forbearance, I blurted: "Wait a minute! Did it ever occur to you that there might be some advantage to being married to the woman who wrote *Plaintext*?" At last I'd reached the point where I could ask that question. But as I sipped coffee and nibbled a chocolate cookie in the company of these polite and pleasant but plainly distressed strangers, my chances of getting an affirmative answer seemed as remote as ever. In this tale, I was decidedly not the Princess but the Dragon.

George has conspired in his own sanctification. Why wouldn't he? The veneration of others must be seductive. And if, in order to perpetuate it, he had to affirm—to me, and through me to others familiar with my writings—his faithfulness even as he shuttled between Sandra and me, well, what harm was he doing? For her own reasons, Sandra was just as eager as he to keep the affair clandestine. They seldom went out and never got together with friends; he never even encountered her child, who was always, magically, "not there"; she'd even meet him in a parking lot and drive him to her house so that the neighbors wouldn't see his car. He could maintain this oddly hermetic relationship without risk to the sympathy and admiration of friends, family, and book reviewers alike. No one need ever know.

Until, ultimately, me. That is, I don't need to know, not at all, I've done very well indeed without knowing, but he has come to need to tell me. At first, he thought merely breaking with Sandra would calm the dread his father's death and the discovery of melanoma in a lymph node stirred in him, but now he needs a stronger remedy. "I feel this awful blackness inside. I just want to die," he says after confessing, and I shudder, because an awful blackness is precisely what he has inside—a six-centimeter melanoma attached to his small bowel—and I don't want him to die, he can tell me anything, I'll accept whatever he confesses, any number of awful blacknesses, if only please he won't die. He hasn't any control over that, alas, but at least now he has cleared his conscience thoroughly. I think he's after another clarity as well, one that involves putting off sainthood and standing naked—bones jutting under wasted flesh, scars puckering arm and belly, penis too limp now for love—as a man. He wants to be loved as he is, not as we—his mother, my mother, my sisters, our daughter, his students, our friends, maybe even Sandra herself—have dreamed him. I most of all. I look anew at the reviewer's words: "The reader will wish to *see more closely* some of the people who *simply drift* through these essays. . . . "

George is accustomed to holding himself slightly aloof. The only child of adoring parents, he grew up believing himself entitled to act on his own desires without regard for the needs of others: There weren't any others. If he wanted the last cookie, it was his. (In fact, even if he didn't want it, his mother probably made him take it.) No noisy wrangles, no division of the coveted cookie followed by wails that "he got the bigger half," no snitching a bite while the other's head was turned or spitting on the other's half to spoil it for both, just complacent munching down to the last sweet crumb. But, by the same token, no whispers and giggles under the covers after Mother has put out the light *for absolutely the last time.* No shared cookies. No shared secrets, either. No entanglements, true. But no intimacy.

Having grown up in an extensive family linked by complicated affections, with a slightly younger sister who still sometimes seems hooked into my flesh, I don't think I ever quite comprehended George's implacable self-sufficiency. Maybe for that reason I allowed, even encouraged, his remoteness. And I did. The reviewer is talking, after all, not about George's nature but about my essays. If the reader wants to "see" George "more closely," then I have not seen him closely enough. George "drifts" through my essays because I permitted him to drift through my life. "I couldn't imagine," he tells me now, "that what I was doing, as long as I kept it in a separate little box, had any effect on the rest of you." Like his indulgent mother, I let him persist in such manly detachment. I'd have served him better as a scrappy sister.

What I might have thought of, in good aging-hippy fashion, as "giving him space," letting him "do his own thing," strikes me now as a failure of love. Respecting another's freedom does not require cutting him loose and letting him drift; the lines of love connecting us one to another are stays, not shackles. I do not want to fail again. After the children and I have each spoken with him separately about the affair, I say to him: "You may have hoped, in confessing to us, that we'd punish you by sending you away, but now you see that we won't do that. If you want to leave, you'll have to go on your own initiative. As far as we're concerned, you're not an only child, you're one of us. We love you. We intend, if you will let us, to keep you."

"You will love me?" George asked at the beginning of this terrible test, and I find, to my relief, that I can keep my promise. "But can you forgive him?" asks our friend Father Ricardo when we seek his counsel, and I reply, without hesitation, "I already have."

I *have*? How can this be? I have never felt more hurt than I do now. I am angry. I am bitter. I try to weep but my eyes feel blasted, although occasionally I shudder and gasp in some stone's version of crying its heart out. I dread going out into the city for fear I'll encounter Sandra. I torment myself with images of George pressing his lips to hers, stroking her hair, slowly unbuttoning her blouse, calling her "sweetheart," too. *She got the sex,* I reflect sardonically as I keep my vigil through surgery and its horrific aftermath, then through chemotherapy, *and I get the death.* I despise her for her willingness to risk my marriage without a thought; and yet in a queer way I pity her because, as it has turned out, she has to live without George and, for the moment, I do not.

Worst of all, ghastly congratulatory cheers ring in my head: *Good-o, George! You've finally given the bitch her comeuppance: tit for tat, an eye for an eye, and not a whit more than she deserves.* "What do you care what people think?" he shrugs when I tell him of this fantastic taunting, but the truth is that, with new comprehension of the suffering my adultery must have caused him, I'm tempted to join the chorus. Still, although our affairs may be connected chronologically (mine all took place before his) and causally (bitterness about mine offered him permission for his), morally they stand separate. I don't merit the pain I'm now in, any more than George ever deserved to be hurt, but we have unquestionably wounded each other horribly and we each bear full moral responsibility for the other's pain. George is right to dismiss my demonic chorus: What matters is not mockery and blame, whether our own or others', but mutual contrition. Over and over when he clings to me and weeps as I cannot and says, "I'm sorry, I'm sorry," I hold him, stroking his back and murmuring reassurances: that I love him, that I'll be all right, that he hasn't "spoiled" us, that through this pain we can grow. Forgiveness is not even in question. It is simply, mysteriously, already accomplished.

Week after week he has stood beside me telling me what I have not wanted to know: *I confess to Almighty God, and to you, my brothers and sisters, that I have sinned, through my own fault, in my thoughts and in my words, in what I have done and in what I have failed to do*. Now that he's divulged the specific contents of his conscience to me, I'm curious what this little ritual of general confession meant during the time he so plainly wasn't sorry for what he was doing. "Did you ever think about Sandra as you said those words?" I ask. "Did you think what you were doing might be wrong?"

"Well, yes, I knew it was. But I also knew I didn't intend to stop. So I just had to hope that God had a sense of humor." Fortunately for George, God has a much better sense of humor than I do. But I've been working on it. Meanwhile, week after week his voice has spoken aloud at my side: *And I ask Blessed Mary ever virgin, all the angels and saints, and you, my brothers and sisters, to pray for me to the Lord our God*. As bidden, I have prayed for him, as for myself and for all the disembodied voices floating up behind me, that God might have mercy on us, forgive us our sins, and lead each one of us to everlasting life. Believing myself forgiven by God, I must believe George equally forgiven. And if forgiven by God, surely no less by me.

One of the elements that drew me into the Catholic Church was the concept of grace, although I've never been able to make more than clumsy sense of it. I am moved by the idea that God always already loves us first, before we love God, wholly and without condition, that God forgives us even before we have done anything to require forgiveness, as we will inevitably do, and that this outpouring of love and forgiveness fortifies us for repentance and reform. I am moved—but not persuaded. I am simply incapable of grasping an abstraction unless I can root it experientially, and nothing in my experience has revealed quite how grace works. Until now. The uncontingent love and forgiveness I feel for George, themselves a gift of grace, unwilled and irresistible, intimate that grace whose nature has eluded me.

For the most theologically unsophisticated of reasons, involving a dead father who went, I was told, to heaven up in the sky, together with continual reiterations, from about the same age on, of "Our Father, who art in heaven . . . ," I always expect spiritual insights to shower like coins of light from on high. When instead they bubble up from the mire like will-o'-the-wisps, I am invariably startled. Grace *here*, among these lies and shattered vows, sleepless nights, remorse, recriminations? Yes, precisely, here: Grace.

But forgiveness does not, whatever the aphorism says, entail forgetfulness. Never mind the sheer impossibility of forgetting that your husband has just told you he's had an affair, a strenuous version of that childhood game in which you try, on a dare, *not* to think about a three-legged green cat licking persimmon marmalade from the tip of its tail. Never mind memory's malarial tenacity, the way that, weeks and months and even years after you think the shock has worn off, as you recall a trip you made to Washington to receive a writing award, it occurs to you that in your absence they may have made love for the first time and all your words, the ones you'd written before and the ones you've written since, shrivel and scatter like ashes. Never mind.

Mind what matters: his presence here, for now. Love is not love, forgiveness is not forgiveness, that effaces the beloved's lineaments by letting him drift, indistinct, through the lives of those who claim him. That way lies lethargy, which is the death of love. I am not married to Saint George, after all. I am married to a man who is, among many other things neither more nor less remarkable, an adulterer. I must remember him: whole.

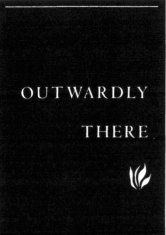

OUTWARDLY THERE

Although from the sense of returning I feel each time I cross myself at the beginning of Mass in the name of the Creator, the Redeemer, and the Holy Spirit, I sometimes think that I was born Catholic into a Protestant family, I certainly wouldn't have seen my situation in those terms at the time I was growing up. Catholic families bore permanently Catholic children, and generally a great many too many of them, and Protestant families bore permanent Protestants. A Catholic was not something one could turn into, any more than one could grow a penis or deepen the pigmentation in one's skin beyond the Coppertoned glister that required an entire summer of New England's fickle sun to achieve, and no spiritual mix-up, akin to the accidental switching of infants in a hospital nursery, was possible. God kept careful track of who belonged to whom.

And so did we. There were Catholics in the small, still almost rural village on the North Shore of Massachusetts where we moved—Mother, Sally, and I together with Granna, Mother's mother—when I was nine. The first Jew didn't move in until I was in college, but the Catholics were already there. We knew who they were. On Thursday afternoons when my fifth-grade class trooped across the street to the American Legion hall for our religion class, Robby Burke stayed behind because the pope wouldn't permit him to think for himself. Maybe not, but he certainly had ample time for thinking *by* himself, while the rest of us crayoned Joseph's coat of many colors and learned not to covet our neighbors' oxen or asses, though in fact my neighbor, the portly, bald school-bus driver known to everyone as Uncle Sid, kept nothing but chickens. I don't remember "studying" religion as a school subject, even on private premises, after fifth grade. Perhaps questions about the separation of church from state surfaced even in this community settled by Puritans in 1636, or perhaps the study of religion was confined to ten-year-olds.

Catholics could live in Enon, but they had to go to church across the line in Hampstead. There was also a Carmelite Junior Seminary atop a hill there—at night a lighted cross crowning a tall spire floated against the sky—but the boys weren't allowed out and none of us ever went up there except my mother the time the police told her the monks had found our lost dog, Pegeen. Episcopalians went to church in Hampstead, too, but we didn't know them since they belonged to the "hot-potato" crowd—so dubbed for their affectation of upper class English vowels—who lived on large estates and sent their children first to Shore Country Day and then to boarding school. One of these estates, Penguin Hall, was later bought by the Catholic Church for a convent and hastily renamed, but not before the townspeople had a good laugh at the bustling black-and-white figures who took it over.

The only two churches in Enon were ours—the First Church in Enon, Congregational—and the church of a community of Baptists Mother called "hard-shelled," meaning that they didn't drink, smoke, dance, play cards, or go to movies, these abstentions signifying a grudging and joyless attitude toward life. Except for our next-door neighbors, I didn't know any of them, and I never set foot in the church, even though it was an easy walk from our house, miles closer than the Congregational one up town, and every day throughout high school the smelly yellow bus picked me up and dropped me off directly in front of it. Because Enon was too small to have its own high school, we could choose either to attend Hampstead High or to be bused to Berkeley, the small city to the south. In my ninth-grade class, some Catholics and Baptists and others with indeterminate affiliations may have gone to Hampstead—at least, they disappeared from view after graduation from junior high—but nobody from our church did.

A three-year high school with about fifteen hundred students, BHS threw me into a broader acquaintanceship than I'd had before. I think there were even a couple of black students, although my sense of them is so dim that my memory may be pulling one of its creative tricks on me. There was a large Catholic community, predominantly Italian, and a good-sized Jewish community as well. I had friends from both groups and felt neither more nor less distant from them than I did from anyone else, which is to say that I felt about eight hundred light years away from every human being I encountered, especially those my own age, so terrified of being misunderstood and ridiculed that I could scarcely drag myself into that massive, musty heap of grey-painted bricks day after day. I was fortunate never to set my sights on a Catholic boy, but the limits would have been just as strict as I knew they were when I developed a crush on a Jewish one: "I must not, MUST NOT, become interested in John," I adjured myself, because he "is Jewish, and while this does not affect my feeling for him, I am afraid to get too close to him for fear that he would be the one and then his religion *would* matter." He was similarly constrained, I knew—"Oh, well, he is Jewish and probably would not be allowed to date me"— although it turned out in my case not to matter.

A certain ecumenical spirit pervaded the Congregationalists at that time, because they were in the process of merging with the Evangelical and Reformed Church to form the United Church of Christ. Thus, long before I was smitten by John, a Jewish rabbi had spoken at Pilgrim Fellowship, and not quite two weeks later we went to "a wonderful, wonderful Jewish synagogue service with Israeli folk singers afterward." We had no such direct contact with the Catholics. I don't suppose they'd have wanted it any more than we. But our minister "did an excellent talk on Catholic-Protestant relations—the similarities and differences between the two faiths"; later, he "spoke on mixed marriages—a very impressive and convincing explanation." Clearly, I didn't need to state the nature of the conviction so readily implanted, but I'll tell you now: Mixed marriages were doomed. Marriage to a Democrat would bring trouble enough (assuming one could find a Congregationalist Democrat)—but to a Catholic or a Jew? "Opposites attract," Mother and Granna were fond of intoning, "but not for long." Like magnets turned wrong end to, partners from different backgrounds were bound to burst apart in an agony of repulsion.

The class demarcations inscribed by these carefully distinguished communities were wholly lost on me, of course. That's the force of class demarcations, isn't it: that they're as invisible as air, and seem as necessary. We were forever sorting people, like socks from a laundry basket, sometimes sight unseen, on the basis of a name (a Genovese was not a Cohen was not an O'Hare, and none of them were us) or place of origin (more than the distance of a few miles separated Peabody or Lynn from Enon or even Hampstead), sometimes by a glimpse of a turned-up collar and tight black skirt ("cheap, cheap!") or even a nose. Over the years, my life has become such a scramble of blond children and children with green or purple hair (or sometimes both at the same time) or no hair at all, of Latinas and lesbians and homeless people with and without their wits about them, of people in wheelchairs and people on canes and people who walk and even run without visible means of support, that I'd go nuts if I continued the elaborate sorting and labeling I learned in childhood, and so I've half-forgotten the shelter and social certainty these exclusions conferred.

In our view, we were not snobs, like those people named Snooky or Buffy with their groundskeepers and polo ponies and even a Basset hound named Fred who was driven home in the town taxi whenever he strayed off his estate. Within the bounds of good taste, which demanded a certain distance, we were relentlessly kind to people less enlightened, by native intelligence and/or education, than ourselves; and I can remember suffering horribly in the company of Shari Muller, a fat, homely, slightly dull classmate from The Pond, Enon's modest ghetto, whose admiration Mother required me to reward by an invitation to our house for an afternoon of play.

In strictly economic terms, my family may have been closer to Shari's than to the families of the girls I went to Sunday School with, since Mother was a young widow living on a government pension and then the wife of a bank manager with two new babies to support. But as the graduate *cum laude* of a small private liberal arts college for women, who had been married to a naval officer and traveled widely, she could more than hold her own among the burghers of the Congregational community. I may have been embarrassed more than once to go to Sunday School and later Pilgrim Fellowship wearing last year's coat, now too short to cover the hem of my secondhand dress, but I never questioned whether I belonged there. Or whether "there" was exactly the right place to be.

I had always been a Congregationalist. Mother had not, having started out an Episcopalian in rather privileged circumstances in Marblehead, but by the time Granna divorced her wealthy but errant husband and moved in with her immigrant parents in Danvers, the family had changed. Granna was originally a Lutheran, and when she tried to join the Congregational Church, she was refused the letter of transfer which would automatically have made her a member. "Once a Lutheran, always a Lutheran," she was told, an attitude that was held up to us as a model of the pigheadedness other denominations were prone to. Of course she joined anyway—Congregationalists aren't sticky about such matters—and so I suppose she wound up with a sort of religious dual citizenship.

I, however, was baptized when I was six months old by the Reverend Paul S. McElroy at the Maple Street Congregational Church in Danvers, I discover between the scuffed pink leather covers of my baby book. One of my earliest memories is of being dressed for Sunday School by my father one morning when Mother was sick. After Daddy died and we moved from the South Pacific to Exeter, New Hampshire, I was sent to Sunday School there so faithfully that I earned pins for perfect attendance, even going to classes among strangers, on the rare occasions we left town, so that my perfection would remain unblemished. An early snapshot, taken in front of the tall, creamcolored church, shows Sally and me with our baby cousin Sam, holding the potted geraniums given us on Children's Sunday. For a while I even sang—rather tunelessly, I'm afraid—in the Junior Choir, less out of a desire to give glory to God than out of delight in the maroon cassocks and crisp white surplices we got to wear. Already I was taken by trappings.

As soon as we moved to Enon, when I was in the fifth grade, we joined the church there, and gradually it began to suck up my time and energies nearly as ferociously as school did. By the time of my first surviving diary, begun while I was in the ninth grade, my pattern of religious practice (by which I mean only those activities related to the church itself, although I belonged also to Girl Scouts and Rainbow Girls, both with patently Protestant Christian overtones in those days) was firmly established. Along with Mother, I had joined the church choir, even though I wasn't crazy about our plain maroon robes, styled like graduation gowns with small white collars; and we practiced every Tuesday evening. On Sunday I went to Sunday School without fail, even though attendance was no longer rewarded with pins, and then sang at the morning worship service. The youth group, Pilgrim Fellowship, met on Sunday evening, and as an officer I often had a planning meeting to attend in the afternoon. Almost any Sunday I flip to tells essentially the same tale:

> *January 12, 1958.* What a day! Is Sunday busy! I went to Sunday School and church, after making pancakes for breakfast. After dinner, at 2:30, Dave called and asked me to go to an Association Meeting at 3:00. What a rush! After the meeting, talked with Dick about my sermon. It's going to be no cinch. Then from there to Bessie Buker School for game night at P.F. Whew!

This basic structure was subject to baroque embellishment, especially during the Christmas and Easter seasons. The young people always put on a Christmas pageant, for instance, and I took my turn as shepherd, angel, wise man; wracked by adolescent angst, I wanted to be the wise man who sang, "Myrrh is mine, its bitter perfume/ breathes a life of gathering gloom," but I got stuck with frankincense instead. Extra services required extra choir practice. And then there were all the ancillary activities: church fairs, covered dish suppers, dedication of the new organ, receptions for ministers and assistants departing and arriving. And this bustle doesn't include Pilgrim Fellowship, which sponsored, in addition to Sunday's meeting, Workdays for Christ, whereby the townspeople got their leaves raked and their storm windows washed and their cellars cleaned out for God's sake; field trips at once edifying and entertaining, among them one to Boston to see *Ben Hur* and another to Harvard to see e.e. cummings's *santa claus*, I recall; and innumerable purely social events like beach picnics, hayrides, sock hops, and more formal dances, at one of which (on Valentine's Day) I succumbed to the second great love of my life (the first, whose family drove a Corvette and lived in a thirty-eight-room house, must have been an Episcopalian). If idle hands do indeed make work for the devil, he must have found little enough to do at the First Church in Enon, Congregational.

Religious practice, then, called for turning one's face outward to one's fellows rather than inward to one's conscience or even upward to God. It was during the post-service ritual of exchanging greetings ("passing the peace" during the service would have seemed revoltingly intimate) that my father's mother, Garm, instructed me in keeping my head up, speaking clearly, and shaking the gloved hand proffered me firmly, not "like a dead fish," a lesson no less serious—and a lot more durable, it would turn out—than the one the minister had just imparted in his sermon on "The Carpenter and the Goldsmith." At times the emphasis on decorum was so relentlessly social that I missed the spiritual connection altogether, and I'll bet everyone else did, too. Mother would have hooted if I'd considered my white cotton gloves, which were supposed to be spotless, an outward and visible sign of an inward and spiritual grace, or if I'd referred to the finery we assembled before Easter—my red Capezio flats, say, or that pink straw hat with the floppy scalloped brim—as resurrection garments (and she still will just as soon as she reads this). Public gestures were made, without reference to God, so that others would have no grounds for criticism of our personal habits.

In some contexts, such an emphasis on propriety could have stifled spiritual autonomy as it stifled social nonconformity. But we were Protestants, remember, historically suspicious of centralized religious authority. Like it or not, our identity whispered *protest*. This subversion at the root didn't matter a whit to the Congregationalists of old, who were called Puritans and who shunned or whipped or even hanged those who deviated from beliefs and behaviors as strictly codified as though the pope himself had decreed them. Congregationalists three centuries later, though hardly freethinkers, were markedly less severe. As long as a young person complied with basic social requirements (didn't wear scarlet lipstick to church or speak rudely of Rupert Lilly's performance on the organ even though he was apt to slide his hands one key to the side and, stone deaf, persist with all the stops out in a rendition of "A Mighty Fortress Is Our God" worthy of John Cage), she was free to struggle with matters of religious conviction and to demur, if not quite to dissent, when receiving wisdom. "Because I said so" provided adequate reason for her being compelled to sit still and not stare at her boyfriend in church but not for her believing that Jonah actually stumbled around for three days in the blackness of a whale's belly. Form was prescribed. Belief she'd have to arrive at on her own.

The process of religious formation, as I was experiencing it, is encapsulated in my sermon for Youth Sunday the winter I was sixteen. Once a year, some Pilgrim Fellowship members were invited to conduct the morning's worship, and I preached in both 1958 and 1960. About the first I noted only the subject—Where Is God?—and that "everyone loved it, and I was so happy. I was really petrified, but I was okay once I started. I hope it pleased God as it did His children. I think it did." The sermon itself has vanished, and I'm a little sorry because I'd love to know Where God Was. For some reason the second one has survived, typed with pale ribbon on sheets of cheap paper bound with a rusted paperclip. "If we young people are to be accepted as adults," it begins, "then we must form adult ideas and opinions," moving "from the childish acceptance of all beliefs . . . through doubt and questioning to form a faith: individual yet ever-growing." The climactic insight I achieve at this point in my progress toward spiritual maturity, that "youth has a religion of its own—worship of beauty, of self, of life"— which will "only logically" lead to the worship of God, suggests that adulthood still lies some way off.

The responsibility for speaking publicly about matters of belief could be anxious-making for a girl aspiring to be "good," and my uneasiness may account for the slightly hysterical edge to my tone and the hubris with which I presumed to speak for my generation, even though, to be honest, I hadn't consulted any other "young people" about the development of their beliefs. We just didn't talk about such things. In selecting me to deliver one of the day's sermons, the minister had thrust me into a position of authority even more alien to me than to the young man who gave the other, since every sermon either he or I had ever heard had been preached by a man; and I overcompensated.

My situation as a woman was anything but clear, not just to me but to the church as a whole, I think. Some points—

like chastity—remained nonnegotiable. But the range of social roles women might choose had begun to broaden. True, only men could be ministers, and many a congregation stayed afloat on the unpaid labor of the minister's wife. True, only men could be deacons, too, whereas directors of Christian education were invariably women. But only twenty years or so later, my sister served first as director of Christian education (the liberation of men lagging characteristically behind) and then as deacon of the selfsame church we grew up in. The seeds that bore such change were already germinating, though still in the soil's darkness, when I was there. Thus, I could hold offices in Pilgrim Fellowship, I could even be asked to preach to the whole congregation, but without seeing adult women in parallel roles, I couldn't feel sure who I was supposed to be(come).

By the time I delivered my sermon, stranded, a little unsteady, up there on the maroon-carpeted dais, staring down at the adult faces (oh, I can see some of them yet, and did on my last visit a couple of years ago: Betty Dodge, Lois Yeo, Susan Lilly) oddly shrunken from such an unaccustomed height and distance and pallid in the bleak February light filtering through the tall unshuttered windows, I'd already been a church member for a couple of years. The preparation for joining had been arduous, I'm surprised to discover from my diary, entailing a year of study (during which I read the entire Bible, though I'm not sure whether we were required to do so or I was characteristically overzealous), a five-question essay examination, a formal interview with the minister, and finally the confirmation itself, on a May morning long since forgotten even though "I was so happy I cried."

The truth is that I had a good many other matters on my mind when I was thirteen, paramount among them the Episcopalian boy with the Corvette and thirty-eight-room house. And I wonder now why on earth such vestigial rites of passage—

requiring that one know one's own mind—are so often situated at precisely the moment when a more or less tranquil childhood is erupting, with the thunder of an Alaskan ice-out, into the hormonal uproar of puberty and one's mind certainly seems anything but one's own capable of being known. When, three years after my confirmation, I wrote my sermon, I knew that "merely joining the church does not necessarily stop the inevitable; eventually every young person comes to a point of questioning"; and one of the questions that struck me as inescapable was "Who are right—the Catholics or the Protestants?" Thanks to my religious instruction, I might or might not believe in God (on the whole, I did) but I certainly credited the authenticity of such a question: there was only one "right," to which only one entity could lay claim; whichever one got it (the Protestants had a decided edge in my book), the other automatically acquired the suppressed but powerfully present "wrong." The faith of our fathers, living still, was predicated upon exclusion in a manner that, though I couldn't yet recognize it, made me uneasy.

By this time I knew—couldn't help knowing even in Enon—that populations as diverse as "Moslems" and "Christian Scientists," also mentioned in my sermon, existed. I had never met one, but I certainly might. Already I had been in love, briefly but with an intensity that rattled my teeth in their sockets, with an African college student I met at a week-long Pilgrim Fellowship officers' conference. "Ayo and I have become too attracted to each other," I scribbled. "It is too unlikely, too fantastic. Different ages, different backgrounds, different races. And yet we are not different. His color affects my reaction to my feelings, but not the feelings themselves. How could this happen? Why? Is it to test my strength, my will to do right? But what is right? According to the rules of society I am sinning deeply. . . . But in God's sight, what? Help me, God please." Or, if not a test, "is this a lesson in love, the kind of love God gives to all his children, regardless of race?" From the distance of thirty-odd years, I know that it was exactly this: a lesson in love.

At the time, all I knew was that I felt not confirmed but confounded, and my bewilderment made the tone of my sermon defensive as well as anxious. The "doubt and self-questioning" I felt were clearly not the marks of maturity as I had been given to understand it. It frequently suits adults, of course, as it suits any group that asserts power over another, to keep young people at a distance and off balance by pretending to special strength and certainty. I never heard an adult say "I'm not sure that God exists" or "I don't know whether God, if He exists, disapproves of interracial dating or sex before marriage or wearing tight black skirts and popping your Double-Bubble." They *were* sure. They *did* know. And I'd be able to tell I'd reached adulthood when I knew, too. Eventually I'd learn that adulthood arrives at precisely the moment one relinquishes this notion.

In the meantime, although fraught with uncertainty, life was also bursting with multifarious possibilities. Only one of which—perhaps, at this point, the least likely one—was that I would turn out to be a Catholic.

THERE
WITHIN

From what I have read of Catholic girlhoods, I sometimes think I'm lucky that mine was a Protestant—and specifically a Congregationalist—one. Restraint was never my strong suit, and the Catholic Church, especially the Church before Vatican II, seems to have held out a veritable cornucopia of excess. I'd probably have worn hair shirts, or at least scratchy woolen vests, even in summer and gone blue-legged if not bare-footed in winter, made novenas nonstop, scared myself silly with Boschian visions of my inevitable doom every time I shouted at my sister or yearned for my young and sympathetic dentist to put his lips to mine instead of jabbing yet another syringe of xylocaine into the tender flesh between my cheek and gum, and then gone like my friend Maria into a convent as soon as I finished high school.

Within the imaginative limits imposed by the absence of fast days and holy days of obligation, confession and penance, visions of purgatory and martyrdom, I achieved what excess I could. I observed each Lent, for instance, by permitting myself to read only the Bible and books about religious figures. For the most part these were indistinguishable from the historical romances I read the rest of the year, only they were about Barabbas and Hosea and Ruth rather than John of Gaunt's paramour or Louis Quatorze. "Mama thinks I'm getting too religious!" I recorded in my diary, so my behavior must have been excessive enough.

Any act performed with specifically religious intent outside a regularly scheduled church activity might well have struck her as excessive enough. In general, religion was confined to the buildings and grounds at the corner of Arbor and Main Streets and, with the exception of Christmas, to Sundays. In a girl's life, weekdays and weeknights were reserved for schoolwork; Fridays, for babysitting; Saturday mornings, for cleaning the house; Saturday afternoons and evenings, and vacations, of course, for recreation. Far from feeling neglected, God himself would surely approve the restraint and decorum this schedule reflected.

The trouble was that, as Mother may have suspected, I was a bit mystically inclined, and for mystics God tends to know no bounds. I had a couple of truly transcendent experiences, I remember, one on a beach at sunset, the other in the icy radiance of a full moon reflected from the glittering crust of a deep snowfall. Not surprisingly, these occurred while I was alone and out of doors—about as far from Sunday morning worship as I could be. I sought out these conditions as often as my terrifically sociable existence permitted. My solitary meanderings might have all but escaped notice had I not, with typical indiscretion, brought back—and even published—reports of them, like this poem that appeared in *The Breeze*, our school literary magazine, around the time Mother expressed concern at my religiosity:

> Whenever I'm troubled or angry or weary,
>> I come to these woods, so dark and deep.
> I wander along in the silent depths
>> Or lie on the moss and sleep.
>
> In Spring, when the air is fragrant and warm
>> And my heart overflows with cheer,
> And the world shines bright, and everything's right
>> And I'm thankful, then I come here.
>
> In the warmth of the open grassy places
>> Or the cool of the shadowy pines
> I walk or sit, and I thank my God
>> For the blissful joy which is mine.

Well, it chugs along through all the seasons, and into increasing gloom, but you get the idea.

Actually, except for an occasional exercise like this (dedicated to my English teacher, a sour woman with sagging eyes, a pug nose, and wayward bra straps), I rarely made this sort of meditation public, and then only in print. I never found out whether anyone I knew had a similar spiritual life—can you imagine what would have happened if I'd asked the girl eating a roast-beef sandwich across the lunch table from me whether she talked to God?—but I didn't think so. My sense of estrangement left me scared and confused: "School tomorrow. I'm frightened. Mostly of the kids. I'm afraid of being misunderstood and ridiculed. I don't understand myself, so how can anyone else understand me?"

Among the friends I made at the Pilgrim Fellowship officers' conferences and retreats I attended, I felt more at ease: "the kids are united, with a oneness I can't find anywhere else," I wrote, confident of our shared values. Even here, however, the emphasis was pragmatic (workshops on effective leadership and the like) and social (plenty of talent shows and dances) rather than spiritual. We worshiped together at chapel before scattering for a period of private reflection called Morning Watch, but no one ever revealed to me what she or he did during that time. Myself, I tended to wander around admiring the countryside. I knew I was supposed to be "praying." I tried and tried to "pray." But it only felt like those times when you feel unutterably sad and think crying would help so you squeeze and blink and gulp but nothing comes.

A good thirty years later, when I was conducting a writers' workshop, a participant startled me by asking how I pray, and I blurted, "I don't. At least, I don't think I do. At least, if I do, I don't do it right." And at that instant I knew that the reason I don't think I pray (outside of repeating something like the Our Father, that is, which is sometimes praying and sometimes not) is that at some level, often beneath my awareness, I never stop muttering to God. I still don't think I'm doing it right, though. Shouldn't prayer be describable as something loftier than a background rumble? Certainly I thought so on those long-ago Morning Watches, when I yearned to split my skin and leap free of it in a wordless ecstatic communion that would heal all misunderstanding and ridicule forever.

On the whole, Congregationalism fostered a kind of brisk, no-nonsense, take-charge attitude toward religious practice which may have tempered my morbid enthusiasms. All the same, it tended to place a child doomed by her own biochemistry to suffer—as I apparently was—beyond an invisible, inarticulable, ineluctable pale. We simply did not suffer, any more than we trimmed our Christmas trees with angel hair and blue bubble lights or decorated our front gardens with painted plaster statues of Mary-on-the-half-shell. Against the maroon velvet drapery at the front of the sanctuary of the First Church in Enon hung a cross, which, when introduced by a newly called minister, caused about half the congregation to threaten to withdraw their membership. But no dead body dangled from the polished wood. After the hosannas of Palm Sunday we paused meditatively at Maundy Thursday and then slid straight in to Easter's jubilation, so in a real sense there was no dead body at all. The crucifixion was merely a necessary pretext for the resurrection, which nullified it.

But in my life there was a dead body, although I never glimpsed it, and according to some theorists of depression, the loss of my father when I was four and a half could account for my later suffering. Whatever the reason, I did come to suffer, quite horribly. I knew I wasn't supposed to, any more than I was supposed to read *Peyton Place* (which I did) or go all the way with a boy (which I didn't). Chagrined, I tried to conceal my wretchedness as assiduously as I buried my spare tissue-wrapped Kotex at the bottom of my clutch purse, that wholly inadequate receptacle then in fashion, confining my woeful outbursts to the pages of my diary, which sometimes proved just as inadequate. The overflow that erupted, all too often and generally at inopportune moments, Mother dismissed as "Nancy's dramatics."

I loved Mother immoderately, and on the whole I felt close to her, closer than my friends seemed to be to their mothers. She looked even younger than she was, slight and blonde and blue-eyed, and we were often taken for sisters. Perhaps for this reason, to have her shrug off as ridiculous my declarations of a pain that I came to fear was driving me mad stung me bitterly. "I really do not feel well," I wrote. "I do not like to tell Mama, because she has so much on her mind that she just gets cross and ignores me and makes me feel like a terrible nuisance." I wasn't yet anywhere near equipped to unravel the snarls in the situation: that she was a Congregationalist too; that through widowhood she had had her own suffering to deal with in her own way; that my sporadic bawls and bleatings might not have communicated my distress comprehensibly; that even if they did, she might out of fear or uncertainty or just plain weariness (she had two little babies by the time I was in truly dire straits) have elected to ignore them in the not unreasonable hope that, without undue attention, they'd fade away. I simply read her exasperated dismissal as abandonment.

I had no other mother to turn to. Mary appeared briefly at one side of the manger in the Christmas pageant. Except for the New Testament writers, the only saints I knew of were painted statues that Catholics were reputed to bow down before and worship, and I don't think I realized that any of these were women. It certainly never occurred to me that one might seek out their companionship through prayer. The writings of feminists of my generation who were raised Catholics suggest that the teachings of the Church have so distorted the experiences of these women that I was fortunate to have escaped their pious influence. And certainly from my present vantage point I'm glad enough to have been spared any further indoctrination in sanctimony, docility, and self-loathing. Still, I wonder what it would have been like to have grown up pressed on all sides by the spirits of holy women. Could I have felt so stranded?

I've got no more way of knowing than Catholics by birth have of gauging how they would have flourished out from under the watchful, dolorous eye of the B.V.M. All I know is that, in the absence of a spiritual mother, the spiritual father, who lived like my biological father in heaven, ruled my psychic roost. These were distinguishable entities—I addressed one as Daddy and the other as God—but their traits were identical: vigilant, stern, affectionate but never indulgent, disappointed by and not particularly tolerant of any thought or gesture less perfect than their own. "Your father would be so pleased," I'd be told if I did anything praiseworthy. Or, if I'd been naughty, "What would your father say?" God was Father. Surely he had the same high standards. Falling short became my greatest dread and, not surprisingly, my most frequent fault.

Jesus himself, we are told, addressed God as Abba—Father, or even Daddy—and taught his followers to do so as well. This radical intimacy may have been a valuable corrective to a tradition in which God cut an ambiguous figure—part trickster, part tyrant—and one might do well to keep a wary distance. But Jesus was teaching adults, not children, and many of them must have been parents themselves. Perhaps even Jesus was a parent. At any rate, he certainly understood the passionate tenderness children evoke in those who care for them, about which children themselves know nothing at all. For them, the relationship to parents—and, in a patriarchal society, to fathers in particular—entails unilateral power. Abba may provide the roof over one's head and bring home the bacon, but he also lays down the law and metes out punishment for transgression, and the love one feels for him cannot help but be tinged with a terror, if not of his force then of his abandonment, the very opposite of the trust Jesus intended to cultivate. I could argue—and often do—that he should have taught us to pray to God as mother too, but that's not my point here. Since the parent-child relationship, regardless of gender, lacks reciprocity from the child's point of view, the Lord's Prayer might well be reserved for adults, who in devoting themselves to their chil-

dren can begin to grasp the power we have to arouse God's
fierce and helpless devotion.

I don't know when the habit began, but by the time I have
a record of my interior life, I was in constant and decidedly one-
sided communication with Our Father: the background rumble
had begun. Who one believes God to be is most accurately revealed not in any credo but in the way one speaks to God when
no one else is listening. My tone, which ranged from wheedling
to truculent, was always that of a child to a distracted parent.
Just as I asked Mother for my two-dollar allowance every week,
I sought favors—frequently of a romantic nature—from God:
"Mon Dieu [I must have had a French test coming up], je vous
prie de me donner un garçon que j'aime et qui m'aime. J'ai
grande besoin de quelqu'un pour aimer. S'il vous plaît, cher
Dieu, écoutez moi." Mother produced pretty reliably. So, in his
own way, did God, I guess, but sometimes I felt as let down as
though Mother had shoved at me a fistful of francs. "I know I
am being unkind and also ungrateful," I wrote after a short,
chubby boy with a sparse blond crewcut and a lisp began to
court me assiduously, "for I prayed God for someone to love me.
But I wanted someone I could love too. 'Ask and it will be given
you; seek and you will find; knock and it will be opened to you.'
I have, God. Have you answered? If so, I have not heard. Open
my ears, Lord, that I may hear and understand." Despite the
note of humility, I was not prepared to take Frank for an answer.

Instead, I kept up my imprecations. Sometimes they
were all but inarticulate—"Please, God, please. Please . . .
please. . . . "—but for the most part during this period I spoke
right up. I never asked for good grades or high test scores or
money or a new dress or a shapely body to put into it, although
I had none of these in abundance; I sensed I was on my own
here. But God alone dispensed or withheld what I longed for.
The love of a man I seemed helpless to get without prayers, and

I was desperate enough to risk my soul: "Is it a sin to ask for love?" I wondered more than once. "If it is, then I am damned." All the same, "certainly I am entitled to pray for some joy," I believed, and joy could bubble up only from the wells of romance.

In addition to—in return for?—handing out goodies, God expected to be obeyed, and this adamancy complicated matters unbearably. How do you obey someone who fails to give clear instructions? Well, you can conflate his wishes with those of someone who speaks plainly. Like your mother. Directed to be home one May afternoon at five o'clock, I wandered instead with my first love, James the Episcopalian, into a field: "talked and lay in grass—it was so crisp and green, smelling clean and fresh and tickling our faces" as we pouted our lips, alternately whistling on blades stretched between our thumbs and exchanging clumsy kisses. As I pedaled home, "I prayed so hard I couldn't breathe," but God didn't alter the hands of the clock, which both pointed straight down as I stumbled into the house. "Mama said little—she knows it's between God and me—but I can't ride my bike for two weeks, and I'm to meditate on my sins."

Since this was the woman who, not two months earlier, thought me too religious, it seems unlikely that she was the one who construed the problem as involving God, and no doubt the reference to meditation on sins was, like a good deal of the communication in our family, formulaic, along the lines of "handsome is as handsome does" and "the Lord helps those who help themselves." Catholics, I gather, were given long lists of very specific sins, together with estimates of the punishment each might incur, as well as precise instructions for gaining absolution; these, if followed, left their spirits scrubbed clean, at least until the instant of the next sin, which, in view of the plenitude of possibilities, was probably not long in arriving. Sin was feasible for Congregationalists, since Jesus would not have the power to forgive sinners if sinners weren't regularly creating themselves, but it wasn't much talked about. It was nasty, and reference to nasty things was rude. Somehow, I think, you were just supposed to *know* what constituted it, but I was thick-headed.

The trouble with failing to know exactly which acts are sinful, however, is that one can't then be sure which ones aren't. Worse yet, Catholics and Protestants alike consider thoughts sinful as well, most of them the sort of thoughts one is having all the time. Most adults—probably by virtue of their not having been struck dead so many times—sort out which acts and thoughts seem genuinely destructive of their own well-being and the well-being of their fellow creatures and establish a working relationship with what they believe to be their sins, avoiding them as best they can and hoping for mercy the rest of the time. Children are still at the waiting-to-be-struck-dead stage. At least I was. Almost anything I did or said or thought *might* lead—I could never be sure—to catastrophe.

Well, then, what sins might I have been meant to meditate on? The one I now feel sure my mother intended was disobedience, which is a sin only in a relationship involving an unequal distribution of power, wherein one party assumes she has the right to expect the other not merely to comply with her commands but also to suffer if she fails to do so. In an intimate and reciprocal relationship, disobedience might result in irritation or disappointment for the one, regret for the other, but not punishment. Mother might have told me, "I feel responsible for you, and when you don't show up on time, I start to worry. I don't like worrying—it feels bad—and so I get angry. Right now I'm furious!" Then she'd have appeared to care not about her right to make me do as she said but about me, as I believe she really did, and I could have said, "I'm sorry I frightened you," a thought that never occurred to me. This is not an indictment of Mother, by the way, because I feel sure that I did the same thing over and over to my own children (and now I'm curious just which horrific episodes they'll dredge up). We are all too apt to believe that a person who distresses us deserves to be distressed in return. The paradigm of a punitive God only reinforces this tendency. Better we should see God as worried.

If I'd been off playing softball (fat chance) or practicing on a friend's piano, disobedience might have seemed my only sin, since there'd never been a whiff of naughtiness about games or music. But I wasn't. I was lying in the long grass with a boy who made me feel about myself—my embodied self—in a way I'd never felt before. And so this act, these feelings, were tacitly drawn into my sense of guilt. Without question—and without explanation—going "too far" with a boy was as bad as you could be. Because I never knew how far "too far" was (the long kiss? the hand on the bra? the hand *in* the bra?), I always assumed it was however far I was going at the moment.

I never recognized the frightening sternness of this prohibition until, some years later, a safely wed mother, I went to visit my parents. While we were playing bridge, Mother was also keeping an eye on the television serial *Peyton Place*, and Mia Farrow had gotten herself knocked up. "But I didn't think you could have a baby," piped up my kibitzing little sister, Barbara, then eight or nine, "unless you got married first." "Well, you can," Mother said tersely, "but it's a very, very terrible thing to do." That was *all* she said. Barbara's eyes flew wide in the face of unspeakable awfulness. I tried to explain a little, not the birds and the bees, just how it was better for people to get married first so that the baby would have two people to take care of it, but really, how much can you say with Mia Farrow's wretched wailing in the background and somebody waiting for you to bid two no trump?

I knew then, however, that some such unelaborated messages must have permeated my upbringing, too. No wonder I lived in terror of my own wicked sexual nature. "May God guide my footsteps and see that I don't tread on forbidden ground," I wrote the year after my brief, sweet relationship with James—and this about a boy I didn't even particularly care for. When, in another year, Caleb came along—the one I'd risked eternal damnation praying for, my own heart's desire—God really had his hands full. "Tonight Caleb said, 'What are we going to do?'" I wrote after a friend's party. "I wonder. After tonight it will all be different. Because we are very close to the edge and we know it." But we went on inching closer and closer until (can it really have been on a Good Friday?) "it almost happened."

Yes, the unmentionable "it." Even though no one ever referred to the act any other way, the unstated referent was specific. All the other stuff might be frowned on, discouraged, but only because grinding lip against lip, sternum against sternum, pelvis against pelvis constituted "playing with fire"; only penetration constituted a burn. I had felt Caleb's naked penis against the naked inside of my thigh: a mere inch or so to go until ignition. "I know I could prevent it if I wanted to," I wrote of the next—the final—step. "Perhaps I will. Perhaps I won't. Strangely enough that seems to matter very little now. It is the breaking of trust. Mama, who, I am sure, would not believe we have gone so far. God. I wish I did not have to bring religion into it, but I do." And there you have it, that conspiracy between earth and heaven whose severest ban I avoided, at least for this moment, transgressing: Mother and God.

The diary entries, especially those written after I made the decision (prompted by some stylistic bad fairy, perhaps the dialogue in those historical romances I favored) to drop virtually all contractions, are so feverish and florid as to all but insist on the wry tone I've fallen into while recounting these transactions. But I can't quite sustain it without a censorship that betrays the girl who scribbled them year after year, for beneath their mannered prose and predictable adolescent anguish lies a sludge-black layer, not in the least funny, which has muddied my negotiations with God at least since July 25, 1958, two days after my fifteenth birthday and a year before Caleb became, albeit inconstantly, the answer to my prayers, when I wrote, "For the first time in my life I asked God to take my life and meant it." From this point on, the terms of my existence took on an extreme and deadly antinomy: "The longing for love possesses my whole being. I hate it. It makes me wretched and miserable and depressed. I do not find any reason for living. I don't just want to love someone. I want to be loved in return. And if God denies me that, I only want to die."

A four-day span early in 1959, during my junior year in high school, encapsulates my spiritual life. *January 3*: "I have so much to do and no time to do it. Oh God. It makes me so depressed. If only I were dead I wouldn't have any worries." *January 4*: "Last night I had the strangest dream. I was running in flying leaps over a huge field. The sky was dark with clouds and the wind moaned. Suddenly I jumped very high, straining upward and crying, 'Oh, God, how long must I wait? Let it be now, Lord, now!' And then God touched me and I was exhilarated, glorified. Oh, how wonderful it was! It seems odd that I should have this dream, having prayed so hard last night to die. I have wanted to tell someone about it, but no one would understand." *January 5*: "Must I always live on the brittle surface of things, gazing down through the clear ice on which I stand onto the deep, real meaning of life? Oh, God, how long must I wait?" *January 6*: "Let it be now, Lord, now!" The rest of my life would be shaped by these themes: depression; detachment from both human sympathy and life's meaning; an ecstatic, erotically charged desire for death.

Not for many years would it occur to me that the silence greeting my pleas might constitute a response, even a sign of love. In the meantime, I responded to it characteristically with ever more frantic gabble that reached a kind of apotheosis during a brief relationship I had with an African diplomat's son my freshman year in college: "So lonely. There is nothing I can say, no way I can describe how I feel. But oh God let Asa come back to me because if he doesn't I shall surely not be worth anything any more and I want to be worth something for him. I cannot face this world, my God, with all the little people if he is not with me. Without him I shall surely retreat into my world and perhaps this time I might close the door behind me and then no one would be able to get to me and I would stifle in there. Send him back to love me in spite of the fact that he is black and I am white. . . . Is it asking too much that I should want the world changed to make me happy? This is my life and when I die there will be nothing more of it—if I promise not to be afraid of pain, will you give him to me without hurting him? But if I cannot have him without hurting him, teach me the patience to live without him. It's up to you, God. I just want you to know how much I love him." If God was still listening at all (I have the sudden image of my stepfather turning off his hearing aids when the confusion around him crescendos unbearably), I can't imagine how he made head or tail of this rhetorical and logical stew. I assume he thought changing the world to make me happy was a little much, but he forbore saying so.

Extracted from the diaries between 1957 and 1961 and typed into my current journal, these petitions cover page after single-spaced page in a relentless, gibbering wail. Only this one—made by odd coincidence two days after my sixteenth birthday—was ever granted: "Oh God no matter how much I pray for it don't let me die." Not long after the dismal, doomed affair with Asa, on a blind date brought about by the theft of a

Corvair from the parking lot behind the gymnasium at Brown University, I met the man who would turn out to be "the ultimate love I am living and striving for," and not long afterward, as I began pouring myself out in daily letters to him, the diary sputters and falls silent. I doubt the Corvair was pilfered by the hand of God, but the last reference the diary makes to God marks the first turn in my prayers from petition to pure gratitude: "I am in love and I know it. Thank God."

.

TURNING

AND

TURNING

Y ou don't really believe that stuff, do you?" my college roommate asked in her distinctive manner, her words rising and falling in little rushes, almost as though she were choking back laughter, although at that moment, drained and disoriented at the end of our first month of college, we were speaking seriously. Hunched in a straight wooden chair, I squinted across our double desk at her, sitting sideways on her cocoa-brown bedspread with her knees drawn up to her chin and her back against a wall painted just the bearable side of Pepto-Bismol pink. The room was cramped and, in memory at least, always dim, lit by a single tall window partly shaded by evergreen shrubs and a pair of milk-glass lamps painted with ivy. Also, because in those days I was always depressed, I seemed to see all my surroundings through a wash of silvery grey.

Puff was a tall handsome blonde of the sort often called cool, with long painted fingernails and dramatic black-rimmed cat's eye glasses, who came from an affluent suburb of Cleveland. Whether because of her elegant wardrobe or her casual references to tennis with her boyfriend at the country club or that breathy, faintly mocking style of speech, I felt intimidated by her: I, the scholarship student with shoes from Thom McAn, too clumsy to return a tennis ball or dive into a swimming pool, emotionally so erratic that within weeks I'd try (without great conviction or effect) to slash my wrists.

Even so, I said that I did.

"But how *can* you?" she asked.

She had me there. I believed in God, I knew I believed in God, but I hadn't the least idea how I did it. She might as well have asked me how I extracted oxygen from the air I breathed (I'd already gotten the first of many Fs on a biology assignment). The religion course I'd just begun had provided no answer, at least not so far. Belief just happened to you. Or, as her question suggested, it didn't. But no one had ever put the matter to me quite so bluntly before. I'd hardly ever been asked to profess my belief in God, much less to justify it. I don't think Congregationalists do that sort of thing. It would constitute an invasion of privacy, which bears an almost sacramental weight.

I was only startled, not affronted, by Puff's obviously genuine puzzlement, however, and embarrassed that I had no answer for her. We'd gotten into college because we were smart, which meant in effect that we were good at taking tests, which required coming up with a lot of answers, more of them right than wrong and none of them, to my recollection, involving God. Nothing in my education had suggested that intelligence could be extrarational, that beyond the Logos lay another domain, as vast and dark as interstellar space appears to the eye, though not as inhospitable, and that silence in the wake of Puff's question was therefore an authentic response. And nothing would for a very long time.

Meanwhile, in spite of my protestations, I was beginning to distance myself from that stuff I believed. In part this process—nothing so dramatic as repudiation, merely a gradual turning away—was one element in the radical and complicated change of habits which occurs when one leaves one place for another, especially for the first time. At Wheaton, early on, I went to chapel occasionally, but I had to make a great effort to do so, and I never felt as though I were really "at church." Church for me remained the First Church in Enon, Congregational, and I continued to go there often when I was at home. But at school, where I was chronically exhausted and depressed and occasionally hung over as well, I began to devote Sundays to sleep rather than worship. Since I'd become by this time something of an *artiste* of self-recrimination, I'm surprised to recall feeling very little guilt at my dereliction. I guess I never especially thought of God as being at church—any more than he was anywhere else, that is, and rather less than he was in the woods behind my house—so I wasn't likely to miss my only chance to contact him if I failed to show up on Sunday morning.

I was also starting to have my doubts about him, not about his existence exactly, but about his nature. I got little enough out of the religion course I took except, with deadly predictability, a crush on the professor, a young pale man with reddish hair who was also my freshman advisor and who, in that capacity, gave me one piece of information so accurate that, despite my initial protracted and fierce resistance, it stayed with me forever. Asked about my goals, I told Mr. Dickinson that my goal was to be happy (though I forbore, with uncharacteristic restraint, noting that all I needed to catapult me straight to it was the pressure of his firm narrow lips on mine). "Happiness isn't a goal, Nancy," he told me. "It's just something that sometimes happens to you as you work toward a goal."

I gave up on religion midway through the year and fulfilled the balance of my distribution requirement with a philosophy course taught by a man so thin and silvery that he might have been cut from onionskin. Perhaps in my mother's day students had sighed over Mr. Austin, but to me he was just "a pill." After a little preliminary browsing in our textbook (entitled, honest to God, *The Destiny of Western Man*) on the nature of morality, I was hopeful: "Of course it was only a taste, but it was so stimulating and such a welcome relief from Dickinson's do's and don't's. At least we are allowed here to search for the origin of morality, instead of having it imposed as the will of the Christian God. I shall be interested to explore it further." I was fed up with being a good girl under the direction of my daddies in heaven, the mortal and the immortal. It was time I started doing and don'ting for myself.

At the time, I conceived my trajectory away from "the Christian God" as a straight line extending into infinity. Seventeen-year-olds tend to be absolutists, their moral lives digitally coded: on/off, in/out, either/or, up-until-now/for-the-rest-of-my-life. They simply haven't had time to see how screwy life is, at least in Einstein's universe: the way, given more time than a seventeen-year-old believes to exist (say, the kind of time that transforms a Mr. Dickinson into a Mr. Austin), a trajectory curves back upon itself, the way one's soul turns and turns again. As a child I had believed. I would never do so again. I would certainly never come to such a pass as to both believe and not believe—and the full spectrum of possibilities in between. Although very little of my behavior in those days would have suggested such a quality, I was a rational being, I told myself, not some kind of a nut.

Daddy God never quite left me, in spite of my newfound faithlessness. He represented a habit of being so fundamental to my psyche that even the barrage of novel experiences college unloaded on me, shattering though I found them, couldn't entirely eradicate it. Unbidden, his name continued to beat at the back of my mind—*God, God, God, God, God*—in moments of fear, of need, of desire, and occasionally of joy. In fact, he's still around today, a good deal greyer, far less severe, still enduring my petulant pleas that the world be changed to make me happy. For his sake, I hope he's gone a little deaf.

He didn't leave me, but he let me go, as a good parent does. For most of the next seventeen years, at the end of which I would profess myself a Roman Catholic, we had the sort of pro forma relationship people often do with parents nowadays, getting together at the holidays and for special events, telephoning or exchanging notes in between, treating one another with courtesy, even affection, but living apart. I had a church wedding, of course—one simply did—and my children were baptised as infants, one in the Congregational church and the other in the Episcopal church so as not to offend either set of grandparents. Having adopted Episcopalianism in order to avoid a mixed marriage, a state held by everyone I consulted to be dangerously volatile, I attended services on almost every Christmas and Easter and sporadically in between. Our relationship, God's and mine, was civil, I would say, if not always cordial.

If I had had some way of talking about it, I would not have said, during all that time, that I had any sort of spiritual life at all. In church I felt like a hypocrite, surrounded by people who knew something I didn't as I pretended to know it, too. It never occurred to me that one might go to church not because one believed in God but precisely because one didn't, that in "going through the motions" one might not be performing empty gestures but preparing a space into which belief could flood if it were going to (though it might not, ever). Talking about her writing habits, Flannery O'Connor said that she was careful to be at her desk every morning so that, if an idea came along, she'd be there to receive it. I now go to Mass in much the same spirit, but for a long time I thought belief was something you had to bring with you, the way a diligent student totes her textbook and completed assignment to class.

I also went through a literalist phase, when the ritualistic cannibalism underlying holy communion heaved to the surface and tilted me off balance. Eat flesh? Drink blood? What was I, an anthropophagite prowling the heart of darkness? Communion in the Congregational church had never aroused this squeamishness, perhaps because the food we were offered was so patently that—food—the kind you might have for breakfast: little white cubes of Tip-Top bread and thimble-sized glasses of Welch's grape juice cut up and poured out by people's mothers down in the parish hall kitchen. But in the Episcopal church we were given papery wafers made by the Sisters of Saint Anne, it was said, and real wine, alcoholic but very sweet, not the sort you'd ever serve to guests, certainly not first thing in the morning. There was a theological distinction, I knew, between consubstantiation, through which the body of Christ somehow coexisted with the bread and wine, and the Roman Catholic transubstantiation, wherein these elements changed completely (except for certain minor details like texture and taste) into his flesh and blood, but the difference struck me as academic, since one way or the other I seemed required to believe I was eating a man. Now even Congregationalism, which I was sure had never suggested I was eating anything but plain fare that stood for Christ in the most attenuated sense, seemed tainted by primitivism.

And yet, while I was shrinking from Christianity and shuffling off whatever bonds to it I could discern, at imperceptible levels new bonds slipped silkily around me so that one day, when I'd learned to look at matters of spirit aslant in different lights, I'd find myself not hanging weightless in a void but anchored to people and practices in all directions. Of these strands, aesthetic satisfaction had the greatest tensile strength. As a major in English literature taking courses in art and music as well, I was immersed in Christianity at least as deeply as I'd have been if I'd stuck with theology. Geoffrey Chaucer and the author of *The Dream of the Rood*, Hieronymus Bosch and Giotto, the thousands of laborers at Hagia Sophia, at Chartres, the nameless monks of Hailles Abbey chanting compline and matins and vespers, these may be the ones who made a Catholic of me. I should have known, I almost did know when, preparing an independent project on T. S. Eliot in my senior year, I was entranced by St. John of the Cross and Dame Julian of Norwich, that something queer was going on in me. But something queer was *always* going on in me, and I had no way of distinguishing one queer thing from another. I probably just thought I was bonkers.

I had hardly grown up in an aesthetic wasteland. No one in Enon could have. As one drives into the village from North Berkeley, Route 1A sheds its shops and restaurants and rounds the wooded lake once famous for the clarity of its ice, passes the shorn hills of the golf course and the cemetery, and enters a picture postcard: a war memorial in a little common, a white clapboard Congregational church on the left, a white clapboard town hall on the right, square shaded Federal houses lining Main Street, the elms gone now but the maples and evergreens grown huge. In area, Enon is unusually large and much of it hasn't been developed since I was young, so it is still possible, at certain angles, to look across empty fields and into shadowed woods, to smell lilacs and newly mown alfalfa and, when the breeze is right, the ocean four miles away. I spent much of my life there on foot or bicycle, moving through it slowly enough to devour its beauty; even the memory stops my breath and makes my ribs ache as though they would break open with desire.

I thought our church particularly lovely, and I still do. It's a little squat, but the lines are clean, the decoration restrained to two Doric columns at the front, black shutters framing the tall windows, and on the steeple a clock with a black face and gold hands and numerals. In "my day" the stark white of the interior was relieved by dark wood on the backs and arms of the high pews and by maroon carpeting, pew cushions, and a velvet drapery, against which hung the disputed wooden cross behind the massive dark pulpit. For adornment there were a pressed tin ceiling from which hung bright brass chandeliers and a row of carved leaves above the drapery. A severe space, not quite stark. In memory I am sitting in it alone on a May evening, late light slanting across the warm wooden communion table on which I have placed a lighted white taper and a single branch of dusty purple lilac, waiting for my Pilgrim Fellows to come in for the worship service I am in charge of this evening: a still point in the turning world.

From earliest memory, I was immersed in literature, especially poetry. Mother, who had been an English major in college, bubbled quotations inexhaustibly: "Come into the garden, Maud, for the black bat night has flown," she'd say if Daddy wanted us to admire his dahlias or tomato plants; "The world is too much with us, late and soon,/ Getting and spending, we lay waste our powers," she'd often sigh when feeling overburdened; so that I grew up with the sounds of poetry so mingled with cautions about my behavior and comments about the weather as to seem a natural part of human discourse. My aunt—"arty," a poet herself—and her husband were chiefly responsible for my aesthetic education. They had a great deal more money than we, with which they bought first a townhouse on Beacon Hill and then an old farmhouse in New Hampshire, both architecturally exquisite although somewhat haphazardly and humorously furnished. They collected art, not Old Masters but "undiscovered" work like vibrant paintings from Haiti and earthy Scheier pots and wall hangings, at once comic and mysterious. Uncle Kip sang in Boston's Chorus Pro Musica, and I began to attend their wonderfully varied concerts: Britten's *Ceremony of Carols*; Bach's "Madhouse" *Passion*, as Aunt Jane called it to lampoon the pretentious announcers on public radio; Beethoven's *Ninth* conducted for the last time by Charles Munch; the *Carmina Burana*; Mozart's *Mass in C Minor*; the Verdi *Requiem*; Poulenc's *Gloria*. When the youth orchestra my son played in did the *Gloria* and I told him I'd been at the U.S. premiere, he seemed awed; I don't think he'd ever fully appreciated just how old I am.

The literature, art, and especially music I studied in college were transformed into ordinary elements of the life I shared, sometimes for weeks at a time, with Jane and Kip. Today, each time I go through the Mass, I feel a frisson of recognition: I've been here before, I've been here for years and years: *Laudamus te! Laudamus te! Benedicimus te! Benedicimus te!* When I decided to become a Catholic, the structure had long since been erected— not just vaulted ceilings and rose windows and bright stiff Byzantine Madonnas in chips of stone but above all the leap and glide and turn, Kyrie to Gloria to Sanctus, of remembered voices—and I was moving home.

The other influence that prepared the ground for my return to religious practice and tugged me closer and closer to Catholicism seems so different from aesthetic gratification, as different as garlic from sapphires, that I don't know how to reconcile the two: my erratically increasing awareness of and commitment to social justice. Perhaps they can't be reconciled, the one so private, contemplative, the other relentlessly public, insisting on action. Perhaps I am simply consigned to practice both however ridiculous I look, like a woman trying to walk with a modicum of grace in one glass slipper and one wooden clog. Or perhaps I simply haven't yet learned enough about reconciliation.

Once, when my brother was about twelve and spending a couple of days with George and me in our third-floor apartment in the center of Waltham, surely one of Massachusetts' ugliest cities, he looked across at the crumbling stucco house next door. "Nancy," he asked meditatively, "is this what they call a slum?" It wasn't, but well he might ask. His knowledge of slums was just as academic (he'd been reading about them in social studies) as mine would have been at his age. I knew there were poor people. We put our old clothes in bags for the Morgan Memorial, the local Goodwill. "Give that to the Morgans," Mother would say as we sorted through our wardrobes for outgrown garments every fall and spring, as though they were a family we knew like the Moffetts or the Moodys, but really they weren't.

In a way, my life has taken the form of a search for the Morgans. Not that I set out to look for them. If anything, I resisted that route. The work of Pilgrim Fellowship, for instance, was carried out by three commissions organized around the themes Faith, Fellowship, and Action, but I belonged only to the Faith Commission, serving as chairman at both the local and regional levels. A worship service I could organize, but sock hops and Workdays for Christ equally gave me the willies. I wasn't entirely unaware of the world beyond Enon: "Yesterday the Russians landed a rocket on the moon," I wrote on September 14, 1959. "Again they have beaten us. . . . Now more than ever we need God and His love." But I had no sense that Nancy and her love would do: "God! what a mess this world is! You have no idea. I want to help. But I can't because I'm too young and I need help. I can't get it even from God."

The frustration of the ineffectual child gave way in college to the apathy so often fostered by privilege, and I suppose I might have devoted the rest of my days to acquiring the right sort of china and joining the right country club and getting my daughter into the right college. (As it happens, I've got some hand-me-down Haviland, chipped and faded but lovely, my daughter got herself into Smith, and although I don't belong to a country club, my mother does, so privilege tends to take care of itself.) As it was, however, something occurred which, to a sheltered girl from New England in 1963, proved extraordinary. I got married (which in itself wasn't at all extraordinary but rather absolutely inevitable) and moved for the summer to Athens, Georgia, where George attended Navy Supply Corps School.

In some ways, I might as well have moved to the moon. Or, more accurately in view of the ravaging heat and humidity, to Venus. Marriage offers culture shock enough without any other change in locale or routine. A thousand miles from home, among people who couldn't understand a word I was saying, I was ill and bewildered for the whole three months I spent there before returning to Wheaton for my last year, and I remember little about our life there. Except for the sex, of course, steamy and slippery and all but incessant. And the Causeys. And Rosa.

We lived on Oglethorpe Road in a huge Victorian house that had been crudely converted into small apartments. No air-conditioning, no shower, lots of ants, but what could you expect for seventy-five dollars a month, and anyway the bed was enormous. In a pretty bungalow across the street lived the Causeys, a plump and amiable couple who seemed quite old, which means that they were probably about as old as I am now. How did they find out that we were Episcopalians? (Technically, I wasn't an Episcopalian yet, but I meant to be.) They must have been told by the priest who stood one afternoon in a cataract of rain knocking and knocking at our back door while we lay naked and sweaty on our tangled sheets and clapped our hands over each other's mouths to shush our giggles. But how did he know? The landlady? George's Navy records? God surely does move in mysterious ways.

Because we didn't have a car, the Causeys offered to drive us to church and on more than one occasion invited us to Sunday dinner afterward: good bourbon brought over the line into our dry county, followed by massive repasts of pot roast and mashed potatoes with gravy and vegetables and quivering jellied salad and hot rolls and sticky dessert, which left us too lethargic even for sex for the rest of the day. On one such afternoon Mrs. Causey, a motherly wrinkle between her eyebrows, asked me whether we swam with colored people in that big pool over at the Supply School. Well, no, we didn't, I told her, because officers and enlisted swam at different hours and all the officers were white. But, she wanted to know, was the pool drained and scrubbed after the coloreds used it? I looked at her closely. She was serious. I didn't think so, but it was well chlorinated, I assured her. All the same, better not to use it, she thought. Clearly, whatever she thought the "coloreds" were going to do to the water (shed their melanin so we'd be dyed black the next time we jumped in? leave their semen so the officers' wives would all bear little black babies?), chlorine wasn't powerful enough to prevent it.

Growing up in suburban Boston, in those years before the Civil Rights Movement, I knew racism existed, but I had never *seen* it. I had known only a few Africans and African Americans, all from privileged backgrounds, and it had never occurred to me that, aside from the accident of pigmentation, they were significantly different from me. But now I could see that, in Mrs. Causey's eyes, even the son of an African ambassador or the daughter of a college professor shouldn't be permitted to swim with me, whereas no one had ever questioned my right to plunge in wherever I liked, and no one ever would. The world was radically different even for Asa and Amanda than it was for me.

As it was, and doubly so, for Rosa, our landlady's maid, a dark wisp of a woman in a flowered apron whom I sometimes encountered wrestling with a giant old Hoover in the shadowy hall as I went upstairs to visit my neighbor. She had to support herself, her children, and at least one grandchild, this neighbor told me, on the forty dollars a week Mrs. Holmes paid her, and if I wanted to give her anything, I should wait till the end of the day or else Mrs. Holmes would go through the sack and keep things for herself. With this caution in mind, one afternoon when I saw Rosa round the back of the house on her way to the bus, I called her in and timidly offered her a beef bone I didn't know how to use, terrified that she'd hurl it at my feet and tell me to keep my stinking garbage to myself.

She did no such thing, of course. Never having had a servant, I didn't recognize the impossibility of such a gesture.

Whatever her private thoughts, she took my foil-wrapped bone, and other things after that. At the end of the summer, when I packed to go back to college, I put my discarded clothes into a sack for Rosa and her daughters instead of the Morgans. Maybe she trampled them in the red Georgia mud or tore them into strips for dishrags. And maybe, if she did, she was right to do so. At the time, I assumed she wore them, and I was glad that, in place of the faceless Morgans, I knew Rosa.

Social activism, however, remained several years away. In the interim, I was making babies. I was establishing a career. I was housebound for months by agoraphobia. I was wearing other people's castoffs until they were too threadbare to give to anyone but my grandmother to tear up and braid into rugs. The world's mess didn't seem to have a patch on my own. Until one Sunday in October 1969, sitting at the dining table in George's parents' summer home in Vermont where he and I had brought the children for a weekend, I closed one section of the *Boston Globe* and saw on the back page an advertisement opposing the Vietnam War. "Better late than never" ought to be my motto, but I often get there in the end. I copied down the telephone number and called the next day to join up.

I can't recall now what caused me thus to set foot on the path that would one day lead beyond simple opposition to radical pacifism. Mine had been anything but a red-diaper babyhood. My diapers had been as snowy as my father's dress whites, which were as spotless as the reputation that outlived him. I grew up fatherless but proud to have been a "Navy junior," born to a man who had graduated eighth in his class at Annapolis, served on the USS *Tennessee* in the Battle of the Coral Sea, taken bachelor's and master's degrees in civil engineering at Rensselaer, swept the last of the "Japs" off Truk to make it safe for my mother and sister and me, died a lieutenant commander at twenty-eight. I've never doubted that, had he lived, he'd have retired an admiral.

Eventually, I got a naval officer of my own. As a handyman at a Girl Scout camp, George, having graduated from Brown without a clue what to do next, was making no discernible progress toward finding himself when an Army draft sergeant did the job for him; and it wasn't hard for me to convince him that Navy Officers' Candidate School would be better than boot camp. The question was, although I didn't recognize it at the time, entirely one of class: I was going to marry this man, and "Army" and "enlisted" were qualities unthinkable in a husband. Certainly the question was not, however, an ethical one: not whether to serve or not to serve but simply how to get through this inescapable duty as comfortably as possible. George and I both disliked Navy life, but not on principle, and were glad enough, in 1966, to escape it.

Socially, the following three years were turbulent, and in spite of my terrific self-absorption during them, I must certainly have been aware of mounting anti-war fervor. But since this was what George and I now call my "forgetful period," during which I was medicated with various psychotropic drugs and received twenty-one electroconvulsive treatments, wreaking havoc with my short-term memory, my awareness may well have blinked on and off like the neon beer signs in a bar window fitfully illuminating a grimy street. Also, although we've known many veterans since, we never at that time knew anyone who went to Vietnam, so the war lacked an intimate face.

Of course, it could be coincidence that I decided to act against the war just a few months after our son Matthew's birth. The construction of my moral life has been so haphazard that coincidence has surely tossed in more than a few bricks. But that was a hard time to bear a male child. Women who had produced male children not all that long before were proudly putting their sons into the ground in flag-draped coffins. (Or—and this may have been a worse death, but we didn't know about it yet—jubilantly welcoming home men who looked like but were not their sons, at least for a while, sometimes forever.) The war in Vietnam would be over before Matthew was old enough to be drafted (it would have to be or we'd run out of sons altogether), but since the government didn't seem to care much where war was going on so long as it was going on somewhere (else), I thought I'd better make that telephone call anyway.

In this way, I met Norm and Lucie Faramelli. You know how easy it is to say, "Such-and-such happened, and I've never been the same since"? In a way, that statement is true about each breath one takes. But in another, very few experiences absolutely and radically alter one's habits of being in the world. My summer in Georgia constituted one of these. The Faramellis offered me a different but comparably powerful shift. Norm, a cradle Catholic turned Episcopalian priest, worked at the Boston Industrial Mission, and Lucie cared for their four children in a ramshackle house in Waltham. One day she told me, her manner characteristically offhand and fervid at the same time, that the Episcopal church there ought to be torn down and the land used to build low-income housing.

About a year after my marriage, I'd been confirmed an Episcopalian by the Bishop of Rhode Island at the little stone church in Saunderstown where the gnomish vicar, Father Dart, had given me some rudimentary instruction. George's parents were terribly pleased and sent me a little red-calf *Book of Common Prayer* embossed with my name in gold, but they didn't drive down; my parents, not at all pleased, certainly didn't; George was at sea; so the only person with me was my landlady. I still have a picture of myself, in the white woolen suit that had been my "going-away" costume with a scrap of black lace on my head, looming among a cluster of girls in frilly white dresses. Over the years George and I went to church, he more regularly than I, generally one at a time so that the other could stay with the current baby, and he even became a member of the Vestry at Christ Church in Waltham. This was his childhood church, and he may have been fond of it, but I never felt part of the community there. Still, even though it was a big space, often sparsely populated, especially at eight o'clock communion, and empty most of the week, I'd never have thought of using it as the site for low-income housing. What a splendid idea!

By this time I knew a little about low-income housing. George and I had bought an ugly old duplex on the South Side, factory housing really, probably built in the days before the old Waltham Watch Company moved to Chicago. We took the eight rooms on the second and third floors and continued to rent the five-room apartment on the first to a family who'd lived there for years. Rents were already beginning to take off as the Massachusetts property tax rate skyrocketed, even in blighted Waltham, and we knew that identical apartments in identical houses throughout the dreary neighborhood cost up to twice what we charged. But the Byrds couldn't afford twice as much. They were good tenants. They were good neighbors. So we left the rent alone and eked out our living just as they did theirs. When the city council held a hearing on rent control, I was the only landlord to speak in favor of the measure. Eking out a living was apparently not a landlordly thing to do.

Well, Christ Church did not get scrapped for low-income housing, I assure you. But Lucie's iconoclasm offered me a new way of thinking about the world which, at twenty-six, I very much needed. With my teacher-husband, my girl child, my boy child, my mortgage, my Volvo station wagon, I didn't have to sink into middle-class respectability, whose soft little paws I could feel all over patting me into quiescence. With Lucie I could collect a pitifully small but fierce group of opponents to the war, use my Thistle stoneware plates to trace circles for peace signs on placards, march these around the Waltham Common by candlelight, wipe spittle off my face, close my ears to the "fuck yous" and my eyes to the raised middle fingers. . . .

War protesters were sparse in Waltham but not in the wider region, and some of us formed a group called Citizens for Participation Politics to draft a candidate for the upcoming Congressional race. One of those bidding for our support was a handsome and articulate young Vietnam veteran named John Kerry, too inexperienced at the moment, we thought, but definitely someone to watch. Instead, we drafted a Jesuit priest, Robert F. Drinan, then Dean of the Boston College Law School, and threw ourselves into his campaign. By this time I'd gone to work full time at the Harvard Law School and George was head of the English department at the Huntington School. Now we were each putting in up to forty hours a week on the campaign. In order to spend time with the children, we took them along with us. To hear our families, you'd have thought we were dragging them into gin palaces or training them to pick pockets. But I don't think Anne and Matthew made much distinction between trudging the streets to put leaflets on doors and hiking up Mount Monadnock (Anne always pooped out and whined to be carried either way), and their curiosity and gregariousness thrived just as well at rallies as at family reunions.

Lucie was indefatigable, but I was not. By now I certainly had multiple sclerosis, and the equivalent of two full-time jobs in addition to parenthood left me reeling. I never regretted my exhaustion, though. In the primary, Drinan defeated an incumbent of twenty-eight years with a high rank on the House Armed Services Committee; then, despite the nastiness of the Republican campaign (rich white men were already smearing their opponents with placental blood), he won the general election. Off he went to Washington, and although we corresponded some on the issue of tax deductions for child care and I cheered him daily during the Watergate hearings, I met this slim, stooped, bald man with the stare of a peregrine falcon, reputed to overrule stop signs with the sign of the cross, only once thereafter. I'm not at all sure he'd welcome the knowledge that he helped to draw me into the Catholic fold. But he might.

Now poverty had a face: Rosa's, the Byrds'. . . . Now peace activism had a face: Matthew's, Lucie's, Bob Drinan's. . . . Mine? Yes. This is how conversion begins, and carries itself along, not with bodiless principles to be embraced by the "mind" or "heart" or "soul" but with a face, a real one, the kind you can take between your two hands and look at long and with love.

IN WHICH

I AM NOT

STRUCK

BLIND

ON THE

ROAD TO

DAMASCUS

I did not set out to be either a Catholic or a feminist, let alone both at once. Although conversion, carried out over the long term, requires deliberation, even discipline, at the outset it often takes one by surprise. But for a set of accidents, some happier than others (and in which some people might, but I would not, discern the hand of God), I'd likely have continued pretty much as I was. Human nature may not require that all points in the known universe remain fixed, or at least wander only slightly and in completely predictable patterns, but my nature certainly does. Major upheaval for me consists in moving the bed from its position under the double windows to the single window in the adjacent wall. I wake disoriented for weeks.

Thus, if the creative writing program at Boston University had accepted me when I decided that the poetry I'd resumed writing in 1971, after an eight-year hiatus, demanded fuller attention, I'd probably have gone on living in that dilapidated duplex in Waltham, attending Christ Church, serving on the Democratic City Committee, clinging precariously, without benefit of medication or psychotherapy, both having been withdrawn, to a life I didn't want without wanting any other. B.U. wouldn't have me. But the University of Arizona would.

Suppose, after we got to Tucson in the suummer of 1972 and began casting around for an Episcopal church to attend, that St. Philip's in the Hills hadn't taken up the collection in large Papago baskets, the price of each one enough to feed a family of four for weeks? Or that we hadn't gone to St. Michael and All Angels on the morning Father Fowler exhorted the congregation to attend an anti-abortion rally that afternoon? Suppose we'd gone the next week instead, when he preached that it's a sin to build nuclear weapons? Might my conversion have been to a more devout and activist Episcopalianism? Well, who knows. After campaigning fruitlessly for George McGovern, I felt dispirited by Arizona's politically conservative climate. I'd only just fallen in with the secular humanists of academe, whom I found terrifically stimulating but detached from social issues, and transformed myself from a technical editor into a teacher of writing (which I didn't recognize as a "ministry" or a "vocation" or any such thing). In this and other ways my life was in an uproar. We bought a house. No, we didn't buy that house after all because we thought I had a brain tumor and was going to die. No, I didn't have a brain tumor but something else, which would eventually be called multiple sclerosis. Since I probably wasn't going to die after all, we bought a different house, in which we would live, for the most part chaotically, for thirteen years.

There just didn't seem to be the kind of quiet time I believed requisite for attending to matters of the spirit. What on earth did I think these were? What did I think "attending" to them constituted? Where did I think they stayed while I drew baths for my children and taught my students where to put topic sentences in their paragraphs and painstakingly translated all the Anglo-Saxon poetry of *The Exeter Book* and made love to my husband and also some other people and boiled quarts of fig jam and took the old, old woman from the bungalow across the street to get her hearing aids fixed and cradled the black cat Freya while she died of feline leukemia virus? So ancient and absolute in Western thinking is the separation of the sacred from the profane that they seem by nature to exclude each other; and so closely are they identified with spiritual and material reality, respectively, that to speak of the interpenetration of soul and body, rather than their (not generally peaceful) coexistence, if one can bring oneself to do it at all, smacks more than a little of scandal. Mystics of all traditions more readily tolerate eruptions of the holy into quotidian routine; but not a lot of mystics go to graduate school, at least at the University of Arizona.

Between degrees, I dropped out of graduate school for a couple of years, however, and took a job at Salpointe, the Catholic high school where George was teaching. This has turned into a conventional preparatory school now, but in the seventies it tried to serve students from the entire Catholic community in Tucson. The practical result was a bit of a hash, as you can imagine, but at least the seasonings included a fair amount of openness to and tolerance for difference. Neither students nor lay faculty were required to be Catholic, of course, and a number of us weren't; the religious faculty were predominantly Carmelites and Sisters of St. Joseph of Carondelet.

I hadn't known many Catholics, not practicing ones anyway, and no religious at all. I'd heard plenty of tales about Catholic schools, of course, of being thwacked on the knuckles by fierce black-swaddled sisters with hairy warts on their chins, the tellers doomed somehow for the rest of their lives to recite their woes as compulsively as the Ancient Mariner, and with as little apparent relief. I didn't expect sisters in tennis shoes. I didn't expect sisters who spent their summer vacations with the farm workers, in the fields, in the camps, in the jails. I didn't expect sisters to run for the state legislature. And win. I didn't expect values to be preached so seldom and practiced so hard. If this was what went on in a Catholic community, this commitment to action, at once light-hearted and dead-earnest . . . then what?

Then what? Be one? How? I didn't have any clearer idea of what Catholics did than I'd once had of what men and women did under the covers in the dark. I'd never even been inside a Catholic church, except as a tourist in St. Patrick's Cathedral and a couple of Spanish missions. We weren't permitted in them, Mother had always said, in the sort of tone that made it clear that we wouldn't have been caught dead in such a place even if the priest had at that instant burst through the door and fallen on his knees begging us to enter and worship his graven images. And he might just do so, since They were always after Us. The more souls the better, and They didn't much care how They got them. Precisely this forbiddenness titillated me as a child. Sometimes, surreptitiously, I whispered the Hail Mary, which was recited nightly in Richard (later Cardinal) Cushing's nasal bleat on the radio, or even made the sign of the cross. But I wouldn't have dreamed of traversing the prohibited threshold. I didn't even look squarely at St. Mary Star of the Sea when I had to scurry past it, merely flicked my eyes sidelong at the grey stone statue on the front.

Mother's contempt was based on a host of misapprehensions, of course, but she couldn't be entirely faulted. If They truly were after Us, They were doing a lousy job. These were the days before the Second Vatican Council, and ecumenism, well under way among the Protestant denominations, was alien to any Catholics we knew. Since, in addition to proscribing our participation in Catholic services, the Church forbade its own members to attend ours, nobody ever got the chance to find out what anybody else was up to. No wonder superstitions flourished. And the stray bits of information that did get communicated tended to make matters worse. "Do you really think I'm going to hell because I eat meat on Fridays?" Mother asked a friend who dropped her fork with a clatter part way through a plate of chicken salad when she remembered it was Friday, and the woman—bright, well-educated, highly placed professionally—said, "Yes." The concept of fasting as a spiritual discipline was wholly foreign to Mother, and possibly to this woman as well. At any rate, no explanation was offered, and Mother was left to contemplate a God who condemns people to hell for eating a few bites of chicken at the wrong moment.

By the time They got Me, Vatican II had so radically, though not universally, transformed Catholic practices and attitudes that I suspect I found the Church as I entered it easier to adjust to than many older Catholics have done. Mine was no instantaneous and convulsive Gnostic redemption. I was not "born again," except in the sense of coming to experience myself as reborn each time I consciously draw a breath and encounter some fresh dazzlement (most recently a pair of tiny lizards engaged in a reptilian tiffle outside my studio door). I entered gradually, without intention on anybody's part. I didn't even have to overcome my trepidation and set foot in a church, only a high school gymnasium, which I went into and out of all the time anyway, for pep rallies and rummage sales and football dances. Masses were held there on holy days for the whole school. I don't suppose I'd have been forced to attend if I'd objected, but I didn't object in the least. I liked to share as much of my students' lives as I could. The liturgy turned out to be structurally indistinguishable from Holy Communion in *The Book of Common Prayer;* the language wasn't as lovely, but the folk music was captivating.

And the wafers were handed out indiscriminately. (Not so the wine as a rule, and the lack has always troubled me, though I can appreciate its economic necessity in many parishes.) The priests knew I wasn't a Catholic; and I'd have given myself away even if they hadn't, since I didn't figure out for a long time that I was supposed to say *amen* before receiving the host. They simply fed me along with everyone else, and I was surprised and grateful. Exclusivity had distressed me years before, when I'd started attending Episcopal services and George's father told me I was prohibited from receiving communion without being confirmed. He was wrong, I found out later from Father Dart, and later still I began to understand that, as the son of an Irish immigrant who'd been raised a Methodist, he was motivated not by dogma but by pride in the exclusive social aura Episcopalianism projected. The social dimension of our conversion, decided on mutually but almost mutely in the spooky way George and I have of traveling, unbeknownst to each other, toward a startling convergence, raised problems for both sets of parents. In New England, Catholics are predominantly working class, many of them the children of immigrants—in those days Irish, Italian, French-Canadian, Polish, and Portuguese—who have continued to be subtly stigmatized by people who go to considerable lengths to trace their lineage to forebears who arrived on the Mayflower (and preferably then to authentic Pilgrims, not deck hands). I have four of these, one of them in common with George, which is not so incestuous as it sounds. In converting, then, he and I were taking a discernible step down; and the fact that, insofar as we thought of it at all, this possessed for us a positive value would make sense to no one in either family.

The model I experienced at Salpointe, then, was one of inclusion rather than exclusion. Instead of being denied communion unless I converted, I was given communion until I felt strong enough to convert. The nourishing quality of the Eucharist, freely offered to anyone who's famished, has always been a central metaphor for me. I don't partake because I'm a good Catholic, holy and pious and sleek. I partake because I'm a bad Catholic, riddled by doubt and anxiety and anger: fainting from severe hypoglycemia of the soul. I need food. "O Holy One," I pray as I savor the host, "as this bread nourishes my body, so may your spirit nourish my soul. Grow strong within me, I pray, and let me live my life in your praise." God doesn't place conditions on the hungry. She feeds first and asks questions later.

One of the questions was (still is, still is): *Will you be a Catholic?* I don't remember now when it began, it feels so much a part of my daily life, but I remember clearly my first *yes.* The day after my thirty-fourth birthday. For some reason now lost to both of us, George and I decided to make a Marriage Encounter at a retreat house in the mountains west of Tucson. This ended in a Mass, after which our large group walked out of the church into the arms of an equally large group of couples bearing candles; these men and women had spent the weekend, we discovered, praying for us. After the prayer couple assigned to us put their candle into our hands, kissed us, wished us joy, we got into our car and wound down out of the desert into the city. In the interval since we'd driven up, two people we'd never set eyes on before, who knew nothing about us except our names and our presence at the encounter, had held us steadily in their hearts. We had been loved by strangers. Something about this gesture, its gratuity, perhaps, clarified a desire we'd hardly spoken of until then. On these grounds—flimsy, some would say, but they've served—we decided to turn into Catholics.

We found this a far simpler process than we'd imagined. Whatever mysteries underlay those casual festivities in the Salpointe gym (and enough childhood superstition clung to me that I couldn't shake the sense that something must have been held back from our Protestant gaze), we weren't required to know them before initiation. We didn't even have to memorize the Baltimore Catechism. Since we'd both been baptised as infants, and a bishop had confirmed us as Episcopalians, we were in effect already Catholics without knowing it. Although we'd left Salpointe by then, a friend there agreed to prepare us to affirm our choice, loaning us some books and meeting with us to answer our questions, but we didn't have many. For both of us, this seemed an intuitive move, the intellectual demands of which would doubtless emerge slowly throughout our lives regardless of the amount of information we gathered beforehand. In a couple of months when we felt ready, Father Bob celebrated a Mass for us and some of our friends in the pretty little chapel at the Carmelite monastery, and afterward we all drank wine and ate conversion cake.

The children accompanied us, but we were careful not to include them in our conversion, partly to soothe George's father's distress that the "last" of the Mairs line (that meant Matthew, since Anne was bound to be given/sold/traded into some other line eventually) would be a Catholic, and partly to conform with our habit of encouraging them to determine their own identities. I've regretted since that we didn't involve them more intimately in our religious life. Not that I worry about their souls. When Anne once told me with the earnest sternness of new adulthood, "I'm not a believer," I could only shrug, "Don't worry about it. God believes in you." Anyone who thinks otherwise—who thinks that, through her own words and actions, she initiates and controls the connection between herself and God—mustn't have much experience of God's boundless affection for even the grudgingest of creatures. But I wonder whether we cheated them a bit. At the least, we could have given them a clearer sense of what they were rejecting when they came down solidly on the side of secularism, in Anne's case, and nihilism, in Matthew's. As my own spiritual awareness deepens and my delight in it grows, I worry that I've carelessly cut off their access to similar satisfaction. Still, spiritual growth may be a function more of my age than of my Catholicism, and they're still very young. I can reasonably hope that they'll find their own routes to fulfillment.

As I write this, I glance at the calendar and note that, by coincidence, almost exactly fourteen years have passed since that evening in the Carmelite chapel when I chose Catholicism for my route. I've gotten into the habit of thinking of myself as a newcomer, but I'm not really anymore. I'm just an ordinary practicing Catholic. Whatever mysteries are associated with Catholic practice were withheld not because I was a Protestant but because I'm human. And I'll need more than fourteen years to plumb them.

By another set of accidents, I didn't convert to feminism until a couple of years later. Aunt Jane, stubbing her mental toe on that locution, writes me in a letter, "There is a kind of woman who has something to do (always known early) and having it to do, she has to do it, and such a woman does not 'become' a feminist. It's more like, if there is a movement, it at some time pulls up parallel to her like another train on the next track." Although I recognize and welcome the acknowledgment by someone who's known me from birth that a gift for language, together with an idiosyncratic personal intensity, marked me a woman with something to do and the drive to do it, I'm not persuaded that these qualities make more than a protofeminist. Something more had to happen to me—emotionally in the form of the guilt and rage such a woman feels when her attempts to carry out her work are variously thwarted, and intellectually in the form of a theoretical structure for interpreting the guilt and the rage and the thwarts as well—before I could adopt an explicitly feminist stance. And the effect was rather less like getting overtaken by a parallel train than like bashing into the cowcatcher of a steam locomotive.

Suppose some happenstance had retarded my progress toward Catholicism or accelerated the head-on arrival of feminism, then who on earth would I be? It may be possible for a woman to start out a Catholic and then become a feminist. Well, it *is* possible, because I did it. What I mean is that it may be possible then to remain a Catholic after becoming a feminist. We shall see about that. But could a feminist—I mean a real, radical feminist, not just someone who thinks that more of the people selling junk bonds and designing stealth bombers and building subdivisions in flood plains ought to be female people—voluntarily commit herself to a tradition that has immemorially and systematically despised her? Some other woman will have to answer that question.

As for me, my feminist development, compared to that of my contemporaries, was delayed by a good decade or so by what I perceive now, of course, as my own resistances. Having graduated from a good women's college (where all but a handful of the courses I took were taught and the works I studied were written by men), I believed myself "liberated" already, unlike those poor creatures who felt compelled to burn their bras. I had a good career (editing the manuscripts of astronomers and nuclear physicists and tax experts, all but a couple of them men). Unlike his father, who hadn't permitted his mother to work outside their home, my husband encouraged me, on the grounds that a job made me "less bitchy." That being labeled a bitch, like absorbing the "greats" from Plato to Pound or tidying up some man's prescriptions for replicating U.S. fiscal practices in Latin America, wasn't precisely a liberating experience wholly escaped my notice.

Whether deliberately or by chance, I didn't develop friendships with the kind of women who were beginning not just to notice these points but to make their observations public. I read *The Feminine Mystique* during the bitter Maine winter I was cooped up in an overheated apartment with my newborn daughter and a pregnant Siamese cat, but I also read all of Sigrid Undset's *Kristin Lavransdätter* and *The Master of Hestviken* and Tolkien's Ring trilogy, and I liked these better. Shortly thereafter, I was so busy developing the persona that would later be christened Superwoman that my emotional energy was pretty well used up. Still, I did find time for friendships, but these took the form of love affairs with men. Nice men, men who clearly valued me for social as well as sexual intercourse, but not the sort of companions who were likely to call my life, including my need for them, into question.

Not long after moving to Tucson, I had a brush with feminism when an acquaintance asked me to participate in a poetry reading at the women's bookstore she and some friends had just opened. I'd just gotten back to poetry and was eager to share my work. But as soon as I got to the shabby little storefront and slipped inside, I heard a woman speak to the only man in the sparse group that had gathered: "You change the energy in the room, you see. Would you mind leaving?"

"Oh, no. No, no. Not at all. Of course." He scrambled up from the floor and bolted. I stayed a little longer, trying to absorb the significance of the scene. Sometimes startlement makes me stupid. Then I put my folder of poems back in my bag and walked out.

What if the young woman who'd brought her friend had been more cautious? What if she'd checked first, the way I'd asked Jody whether I could invite George, and been told, "Better not"? What if the woman who'd challenged his presence had figured that accidents happen and she could bear with the energy change for just this night? Or I'd arrived a couple of minutes later and assumed that the young man hastily reentering the dark street had decided all on his own that listening to a bunch of women read poems wasn't his idea of a good time and he'd rather go up a couple of blocks to Choo-Choo's and drink a few beers?

Instead, I'd heard what sounded to me then—and still does—like the equivalent of "No Irish Need Apply" or "Whites Only." If this was feminism (in those days I assumed there was only one feminism, and for all I knew, this could have been it), I wanted no part of it. I'd slogged through years of antiwar work, on behalf of the men being sent to Vietnam as much as the women waiting for them to return. If I was to be an "ist" of any sort, I'd call myself a "humanist."

And that's the stance I cleaved to for another six years, at the end of which I noted in my journal: "I am trying to think about my identity as a woman and find that I can't really do so. I mean, I can think—a little—about my identity as a person, and that includes gender, but my distinctive femaleness eludes me. The feminists say that I have suffered a great deal because of it. Perhaps. But I have not much been aware of that suffering, I think, but rather of the suffering that comes from being alive. Of course I've suffered as a woman—that's what I am—but is the order of suffering any different from that I'd have felt as a man? Is it stronger? sharper? more exquisite? I can't get a sense of myself as distinct from the other gender. Maybe this is what some men find threatening about me—that I mix myself up with them."

Mixed up I certainly was, though I doubt now that most men cared one way or the other. After all, even though I claimed really to like the idea of having a woman friend and to wish I knew how to make one, I'd "never found a woman I'd rather spend time with than a man." When one of these men, a fellow creative writing student, "told me one day that he didn't enjoy reading women authors and another day that the class had been good because no women were there," I kept silent "for fear that I'll get shrugged off as a bitchy feminist and do more harm than good." Harm to whom? The man who had just told me that the best thing about me was my absence? I was furious when, as a result of my outspoken resistance to a Salpointe principal who struck me as a "mad robot on the loose," I was "let go" by his successor but George, equally opposed, was not. How could I possibly have mixed myself up in any manner with the likes of that writing student or either of those priests?

And yet, how could I safely not? To the extent that I adulterated my gender, I could disguise its force in my life. I was a woman, sure, but since when did that keep a good man down? This bravado, brittle and about one millimeter thick, masked terror instead of lancing it. In the roles that most unambiguously marked me a woman—wife, mother—I felt "sick and empty and scared." If anything threatened to punch through my man-mask, beneath which lay only a vast cipher, as gaping and greedy as a black hole, I ducked and dodged. Feminism promised to have just that punching power. Like a lot of women, believing it the last thing I could afford, I denied any personal need for it. The women's movement had plenty to offer to some,

I was sure: battered women, lesbians, women with unwanted pregnancies, those who were being sexually harassed or denied promotions or otherwise oppressed. Just not *me*.

Still, slowly and painfully—oh, I can't tell how how slow the process was, how painful, but perhaps you have experienced it too, perhaps you know—the mask cracked until, on August 29, 1979, I *tried* at least to think about my identity as a woman. Merely, again, by chance: My cousin had bought from a classmate at Vassar a set of books by Virginia Woolf, which he'd stowed, unread, in a little bookcase in the room I borrowed from him for a couple of months at his parents' farm. I was there to write, so, looking for a "constructive" respite after a morning's work (is any creature more puritanical than a writer?), I pulled *A Writer's Diary* from the shelf. After that I read all the others, shifted my doctoral degree program from English education to English literature, began to study feminist theory, and had a nervous breakdown. After *that* I finished a volume of poems on purpose and started by accident to write essays, a fortuity that would eventually land me in my current predicament, from which God has not shown herself inclined to release me.

I work out my perplexities in a small community, perhaps two dozen at the core, though others enter and leave as their lives permit. After the image of Christ of the Desert by the contemporary iconographer Robert Lenz, which rests on whatever table is serving as an altar and also appears on the letterhead on which we write letters of support and protest, we call ourselves the Community of Christ of the Desert. In age we range from twelve to about ninety. Some are born Catholics, others are made Catholics, and others aren't Catholics at all. I guess you'd have to say we're catholics. Although our backgrounds and professions vary widely, we've been brought and bound together by a commitment to social justice which has required us to confront the inevitability articulated by Leonardo Boff: "A lay Christian, in the light of faith, can and must make political choices, even when these options do not enjoy the institutional support of the hierarchy."[1]

The community coalesced around Father Ricardo Elford, a Redemptorist who for ten years led a weekly vigil opposing U.S. involvement in El Salvador and has ministered to the Salvadoran and Guatemalan refugees being sheltered at Southside Presbyterian Church. Never directly connected with the Sanctuary movement, George and I met Ricardo through a citywide Catholics for Peace and Justice committee. Some members of our community belong to Veterans for Peace, Pueblo por la Causa, Call to Action, Catholics Speak Out, Catholics for a Free Choice, and similar organizations. We subscribe to publications like the *National Catholic Reporter* and *Catholic Worker.* Several of us have committed civil disobedience at the Nevada Nuclear Test Site. Many serve hungry and homeless people through Casa María and the Primavera Foundation. On paper we're no doubt as fine a bunch of bleeding-heart liberals as you could hope to see.

In the flesh we're something else. In the flesh everyone is always something else. That's incarnation for you.

Every other Sunday afternoon, the community meets for Mass in the little chapel at Desert House of Prayer, in the foothills of the Tucson Mountains; in between, it gathers in someone's home for a leisurely Mass, in which discussion takes the place of a homily, followed by a potluck supper. Although none of us have formally repudiated the institutional Church, we all, with varying degrees of anger, seek to distance ourselves from its rigid hierarchical structure, its intolerance toward human diversity, and its inclination to foster quiescence among both clergy and laity in order to perpetuate its own power. Far from breaking with venerable tradition, however, we are stripping away the overlays and encrustations of more recent religious practice to retrieve the plain bare early form of "house church": a few friends (two or three will do) gathered around a table to eat, drink, reminisce, reflect, celebrate.

The United States alone holds thousands and thousands of us "deviates," many far more active and outspoken than I, as an advertisement in the *New York Times* placed by the grass-roots organization Call to Action a couple of Ash Wednesdays ago made clear. More than four thousand signatories from across the country demanded the following reforms:

- incorporation of women at all levels of ministry and decision-making;
- ordination of women and married priests;
- consultation of the Catholic people in developing Church teaching on human sexuality;
- participation of laity, religious, and clergy in selecting local bishops;
- revision of liturgy, language, and leadership to include native cultures;
- open dialogue, academic freedom, and due process;
- financial openness at all levels;
- concrete plans for reuniting all Christian churches;
- a collegial and collaborative style of leadership;
- participation of the people in decisions to close parishes and schools;
- fundamental changes to attract young people who view the Church as authoritarian and hypocritical.[2]

In other countries, especially those in Latin America, even more radical revisions have been called for and instituted thanks to the fundamental tenet of liberation theology: that the Gospels reveal God's preferential option for the poor. One day, the

Church may yield to such pressures and be transformed; or, finding itself bereft of new clergy and religious, abandoned by the laity, impoverished, its dogmas increasingly irrelevant, it will crumple and slough off like old skin, and new life, new creation, will grow in its place.

"But if you've got all these complaints about Catholicism," asks my son-in-law the logical positivist, "why don't you just go out and start a church of your own?" I adore Eric, who has slipped into our family as though a space just his shape had been waiting for him to come along, and with whom I have spent many companionable hours failing to solve the problems of the world, and I can count on him to grasp the distinction I draw between Catholicism and the Church. But how do I explain to this thoroughly secular young doctoral student in biochemistry that one doesn't start churches the way one starts experiments on immune responses to immortal cells introduced into nude mice or turtle bladders, that the search for God differs axiomatically from the search for cancer? The tug—aesthetic, mystical, moral, eschatalogical—of Catholic tradition would mean as little to him as the results of his painstaking assays would mean to me.

"I don't want another church," I say to him simply. "I just want to get this one right." I don't tell him that, as one of the incommensurable differences between God research and cancer research, my desire to get it right is not rooted in the expectation that either it or I can ever be gotten right. He would think me frivolous or pessimistic, and I am neither. I merely recognize, with the kind of resignation forty-eight-year-olds can summon more readily than twenty-six-year-olds, the interminability of institutional as well as individual conversion.

My twofold task.

In the classic narrative of personal conversion, Augustine's *Confessions*, one scholar of autobiography points out, "the self is presented as the stage for a battle of opposing forces and . . . a climactic victory for one force—spirit defeating flesh—completes the drama of the self," a structure that "simply does not accord with the deepest realities of women's experience. . . . "[3] I agree that this model of climax-as-completion appears more characteristically in men's lifewriting than in women's, but I suspect that it doesn't accord with the deepest realities of men's experience either, unless you're willing to essentialize those realities as anxiety about sexual performance. A narrative is not anybody's reality. That's its whole point. It's a mechanism for making something comprehensible/bearable/pleasurable out of a welter of data so raw that even time doesn't exist there. Its function is precisely this: to make time happen.

Narratives possess the shortcoming that they drive toward ends, preferably tidy ones. Some of us tolerate a lack of closure more comfortably than others, but we have all been trained—at least from the moment Mother first said, "Finish your peas or you don't get any dessert"—to associate satisfaction with completion and completion with relief, no matter how pleasurable the tension leading up to it. "There, that's done!" we say, swirling the last of the frosting on the cake, typing "LAST PAGE" on the manuscript, giving the ultimate massive push that pops the squalling baby into the world. These aren't real endings, of course. The cake gets eaten, and then someone says, "I'm hungry." A new idea starts itching the back of a writer's brain until, too distracted to bake a decent cake, she turns on the computer, puts in a new disk, and types page one. And let's face it, babies get bigger but they don't get "done."

Nor, Augustine to the contrary, does a convert end up converted, although in examining my conversion(s) more or less chronologically I may have suggested a settled state as an outcome. This impression is a product of language: a convert, one who "has experienced conversion," is exclusively a product. As a writer, I may define myself as one who "is writing" a book of essays from the perspective of a Catholic feminist. But I can't analogously call myself a "converter" (except, perhaps, in the sense of a "cipher machine" for decoding cryptic messages). There is no word for the convert *en procès*, who is precisely the one I perceive myself to be.

To narrate my "getting here from there," then, is to give my state as a Catholic feminist a substantiality it cannot possibly possess. "Hereness" is extraordinarily fragile, the most fleeting of phenomena, materializing out of dread and desire, slipping forever back there where what's done *is* done. Creatures like my corgi, who is just now savoring the scents wafting past my studio door, may dwell almost exclusively in the moment, but the future overlooms and the past devours the human present. My "here" isn't even the one in which I began this essay (in part because I began this essay), much less the one in which I wrote "page one" or will (will I?) write "LAST PAGE." At each instant I find myself here I must turn again, choose again, name myself again, anew, "Catholic," "feminist," struggle again to fathom the significance of affirming so provisional an identity, ask again the question I put during a period of excruciating loss to Father Ricardo: "How is God here?"

She is. I just want to understand how.

PART TWO

Daily Bread

WEDLOCK (HEADLOCK, DEADLOCK), OR CAN A WOMAN COMMIT HERSELF WITHOUT GETTING HERSELF COMMITTED?

Why do you have to write about *that?*" my mother-in-law asks plaintively when I tell her I'm working on the section of my book that deals with marriage and the family. "What does that have to do with your subject? I thought you were writing about being a Catholic feminist."

"But, but," I stutter, "but I'm a *married* Catholic feminist."

"Well, yes, but I thought you were going to write about abortion and priest-hood for women and things like that."

"Those too, of course. But

marriage is one of the sacraments. How could I just skip over it?"

"I still don't see what marriage has to do with what you're writing about." Her tone is both reproachful and dismissive.

Ah, of course. Because we haven't been together in several months, I'm rusty at the task of listening for her unspoken messages, but now I get this one. I've written about marriage before (although until now I haven't had George's permission to do so freely), and she's hated even my limited personal revelations, which she's hardly alone in finding indecent. A lifelong churchgoer herself, she doesn't really think marriage is totally unrelated to religious belief, or she wouldn't if she stopped to reflect. But her dread gets in the way of insight. *Not again!* she's telegraphing to me. *Don't give away any more of those terrible secrets!*

But how can I not re-explore this bond that has grounded my life since the moment, more than thirty years ago, when I began to dream of becoming George's wife? And I *did* dream of becoming George's wife, not of George's becoming my husband. From the outset I assumed the role of the wretch, the one who needed rescuing and perfecting, and marriage promised, in transforming me from Nancy Pedrick Smith to Nancy Pedrick Mairs, to make of me a new creature. This was, and has remained, the paradigmatic conversion, infinitely more powerful and penetrating than anything connected with exclusively religious conviction or practice. I might have found another way to God. I might have found a better way to God. But I did not. My spirit has been schooled in wedlock.

Perhaps no other avenue was open to a young woman in my social circumstances. My family went to church to find God, but we did not invite God home with us. Sometimes we invited the minister, but even that visit created a bit of a strain, what with the worry about whether or not cocktails could be served and the dread that the cats would copulate on their favorite chair in the livingroom. Except for saying "Now I lay me down to sleep" with my baby brother and sister when we put them to bed and repeating the Lord's Prayer in unison before Thanksgiving and Christmas dinners, we didn't pray in the house. Occasionally, at Sunday dinner as a rule, I'd introduce a religious subject, but these discussions tended to end badly when Mother's and Granna's conventional values collided with my adolescent iconoclasm. As for icons, our house certainly contained none of them (the seven surviving porcelain statues of the Eight Chinese Immortals and the wooden carving of Ho Tei, the Laughing Buddha, don't count, having had sentimental but no symbolic value).

Marriage, by contrast, whether in its absence or in its presence, permeated our daily lives. Although divorce was uncommon, Granna had been forced to undertake that unpleasant duty by Grandfather's bad behavior, about which I learned no details until after I was married; Garm and Pop, my father's parents, remained married, the strains in the union laboriously concealed from us children. For my mother, tragically widowed, everybody's fondest wish was remarriage. Although, with a child's devotion, I thought her perfect however she was, I could tell over time that she was thought deformed in some way, a kind of amputee, and my own life skewed and impoverished by her lack. When she remarried the fall after I turned eleven, I shared the relief of all her family and friends and looked forward to having a real life at last.

This marriage, together with my aunt's, in which I lived for days and later weeks at a time, constituted my model of normalcy, augmented by the flickering black-and-white stereotypes that permeated the consciousness of my generation perhaps more powerfully, certainly more generally, than any medium had been able to do before: "Leave It to Beaver," "Father Knows Best," "The Danny Thomas Show." . . . A lot has been made of the discrepancies between these televised comedies and "reality"—black children watching all-white households, children of divorce observing only intact families, working-class children seeing mothers dole out milk, cookies, and tender advice after school—but what spooks me are the correspondences. I swallowed treacle and propaganda alike without a single skeptical gag because these depictions so nearly matched my own experience.

That that experience might be just as carefully manipulated as a television show I had little reason to suspect. The suicide of one grandfather and the alcoholism of the other may have been the most dramatic family troubles kept from me, but the general policy was to insulate children from all the details of adult relationships. Sometimes there were hints, of course, whispers and then, when you drew closer to make out what they were saying, a quick caution: "Little pitchers have big ears." But for the most part couples denied marital strains not just to children but to friends, other family members, and even each other. One elderly relative claims proudly that in fifty years of marriage she and her husband "never had a cross word," although her son has early memories of his father's raised voice and his mother's tears. The social face of marriage in our world was to remain as bland and smooth as that of a well-fed infant.

In August 1967 I was committed to Metropolitan State Hospital, suffering from severe depression and anxiety, I was told. I didn't know anything about that. I only knew that I felt as though I was about to jump out of my skin. I couldn't draw a full breath. I couldn't stop crying. Except in my husband's company, I couldn't leave our apartment, and there wasn't much point in leaving anyway, since I couldn't enter an office, a shop, a restaurant, a theatre, a church. Only a mental hospital. That was the one place left for me.

By then, I'd been married a little over four years. My daughter was not quite two. I remained for slightly more than six months, during which I almost died once from swallowing an overdose of Darvon, had a flagrant affair with another inmate even loopier than I, and received twenty-one electroconvulsive treatments. My psychotherapists focused on my confused and desperate emotional state rather than on intellectual or spiritual development. I was never educated about my condition. I was certainly never told that the world held others like me—young intense women terrified of flaw or failure—and because my background set me apart from most of the people confined with me, I didn't figure it out for myself. Nor did I make any connection between being committed to a state mental hospital and my earlier commitment, social and spiritual, to an airier but no less confining institution.

On the contrary, virtually all the elements of my experience conspired to obscure that connection. From earliest girlhood my notion of the consequences of marriage, though hazy, glowed with promise; I definitely did not suspect that they could include madness. And my treatment at Met State aimed at returning me, not so much transformed as resigned, to precisely the context in which I'd cracked up in the first place. I don't mean to suggest that marriage was the sole reason for my illness. And I especially don't mean to suggest that George personally and intentionally drove me nuts. George personally and intentionally held me fast with a stubbornness bordering on the nutty, at least by the standards of many who judge us, which is, I suppose, how he got the reputation of a saint, saintliness generally bearing a fanatical edge. The soul of John of the Cross struggled in its dark night. The flames of lust licked at Jerome's heels (euphemistically speaking) as he fled into the desert. Stephen suffered stones; Sebastian, arrows; Bartholomew, the flaying knife. George married me.

But marriage turned out to be in its essence nothing personal. Rather, it took the form of a double helix replicating itself without regard for our particular histories and desires. We dreamed we were creating it ("can we ask any more than that we be set apart under the conditions of unity," I wrote to George during our engagement, "in order that we may effect this unity? What we create then is ours") and all the while it created us: Husband and Wife. Not Spouse and Spouse, mind you, but Husband and Wife, creatures whose differing privileges and responsibilities, imposed so immemorially as to have the force of nature, mocked that "unity" of my dreams, which is prescribed by canon law as one of the "essential properties" of marriage. Easier to unite a boa constrictor and a baboon (unless "swallowing whole" counts as "uniting"). We'd known nothing of the impersonal structure and force of wedlock at the outset, however, and our ignorance very nearly did us in.

Whenever we reflect on the period during which we were preparing a wedding, if not a marriage, George speaks in a tone at once amused and appalled: "Did you have any idea what marriage involved? What did you think it would be like?" I had probably given the matter a lot more thought than he, since girls were expected to, but I had no clearer idea; on the contrary, all that extra fantasizing had probably made me muzzier. In my surviving correspondence, the only concrete detail I report is that I acquired sets of measuring cups and yellow enamel saucepans, so I must have thought I was going to cook. Otherwise, I dreamed in the images in which month after month of the *Ladies' Home Journal* had instructed me: "a wedding and sleeping beside you each night and giving you children and a home and being a kind of strength and shelter to you as you need me." Since I also read the *Journal's* column "Can This Marriage Be Saved?" I also feared "arguments and finding ourselves isolated emotionally from each other and the loss of a child and above all somehow destroying our love for each other."

The baby-faced icon of marriage beaming on us vacuously, we had no notion how to develop and work through arguments, how to reach across the fathomless rifts that would yawn without warning between us, how to ask for and offer comfort. We had measuring cups and yellow enamel saucepans in graduated sizes. Also more and more sterling silver candlesticks as the gifts began arriving. We had about an hour's talk with the minister, during which he counseled us how to avoid fighting about money, which we didn't have. We had between us forty-one years of earthly experience, divided not quite equally, one college degree and another on the way, a commission in the United States Navy, and two healthy libidos. We were going to get married.

What could "marriage" have signified? A legal contract? No, I had no experience with contractual relations; even my student loan hadn't yet fallen due. We had a church wedding, of course, everybody who wasn't pregnant did, but marriage couldn't have meant to me a sacrament in those days; Congregationalists have services or ceremonies but not sacraments. I could never have associated marriage with vocation, a word used only to mean a "job," for which I was quite carefully not being prepared since I would not, except perhaps briefly before marriage, ever work outside my home. I'm not sure I'd encountered the other kind of vocation, except possibly for ministers, who were all men, or missionaries, who were unimaginably remote. Attending college sixty miles from home had caused me enough agony to convince me that I was in no danger of being called to darkest

Africa and needn't even bother to keep my ears open. In any case, for Protestants neither ministry nor mission precluded marriage.

As for whether I might have been called to celibate life, well, the thought never crossed my mind. I don't mean I considered and discarded it, even glancingly, I mean it simply wasn't available to me in any form. One of the strongest anti-Catholic criticisms I heard growing up was that celibate priests presumed to dictate to married people on matters such as birth control and divorce which no experience had prepared them to understand. It was also one of the soundest. But it had the effect of constricting my idea of celibacy to a single negative point: Celibacy was not a spiritual option but an emotional defect in men. About women no one said anything at all, except to recount that my sister, seeing her first nuns, tugged at Mother's sleeve and cried out, "Look, Mummy, black ghosts!" We knew as little about them as we did about any ghosts.

Thus, I never went through the phase described by most of my Catholic women friends of contemplating "marriage to Christ" instead of to an earthly man. Some of them tell me I haven't missed much, that it's the sort of thing one gets over like other childhood infatuations, but I'm not sure that the possessor of an experience can ever quite appreciate its lack. Leaving aside perfervid adolescent piety, what I missed was the opportunity to consider single life an authentic choice. I might remain single, but I would do so only by default, as an "old maid," dedicating my shrunken life to whatever pursuits I could find to substitute, palely, for the husband and children fate had denied me. We pitied such women, the ones who for some reason (acting too smart was a particularly deadly one, but beating your boyfriend at bowling didn't help either) failed to get a man, we didn't revere them.

Stung by a friend's perspicacious comment that what I

wanted was to get myself safely and speedily married, to whom didn't seem to make much difference, I wrote to George a couple of months before our engagement: "if you were to go away, I would not want marriage at all. Not right away. I should want to live by myself, separate, perhaps finish school, get a job, be alone." *Not right away.* Singleness could be contemplated, but only as a temporary state, because I seemed "somehow 'predestined' for marriage (not in an ill-fated way, but by the influences of marriage and motherhood as a good life which I have always lived with)." *A good life?* I would say now: the only life. Whatever I thought marriage to be in formal terms, it afforded my single chance for happiness; when only one road opens through a wood of any color, you don't worry whether you've taken the right one. Behind me lay a lonely girlhood, marked by the loss of a father and the longing for an "ultimate" love to close that wound; ahead stood a skinny man in a morning coat with a sprig of stephanotis in the lapel, his dark eyes wide with what I chose to believe was adoration rather than terror, in whose company I would never feel abandoned again. I fled down that aisle—hoop swaying, ten-foot train rustling, illusion veil floating before my eyes—without a backward glance.

Marriage As Pageant: that's what I understood. The Bride and Groom Beside the Wedding Cake. The Newlyweds in Their First Home. The Proud Parents with Their First Child (A Fine Healthy Boy). Could I imagine beyond that point? Maybe, hazily: First Child's First Day at School, First Child's First Date, First Child's College Graduation, First Child's Wedding. . . . Because the machinery of the marriages I'd known had been curtained so carefully, the future stretched out in silent and almost featureless tableaux, an iterative procession of Thanksgivings,

Christmases, Easters, Fourths of July, that peculiar mix of sacred and secular high holidays which had punctuated my childhood with one disappointment after another, all redeemed, transformed, perfected by George's presence.

The reality this vision obscured was Marriage As Process, not a state of wedded bliss (or, less thinkably, a slough of shattered dreams) but a sustained negotiatory association between two creatures who speak, at best, only pidgin versions of each other's language. I'm not referring here to theoretical linguistic differentiation according to gender, race, class, age, and so on; I have in mind the even more profound idiolectical differences that render each of us (except perhaps identical twins) capable of only the roughest sense of what on earth any other, no matter how beloved, is talking about. "I know exactly what you mean," we tend to say, trying through sympathy and good will to deny the slippage along the fault lines between us, the way we drift together and apart but never merge, our radical insular grief. To be honest, at least half the time I, for one, don't know exactly what I mean, much less what you mean. If I tell you I do, you will expect from me something I can never give: an end to being alone. Better I should tell you I know approximately what you mean. No, not even that. Better I should shut up and listen.

I had this information, at least in abstract form, a year before George and I married: "I want to say to you everything I am thinking and feeling, and I tell you as much as I can transpose to my tongue, but the inside of me is estranged from everyone, even you, and even when I think I can talk about something, it often becomes twisted around sound and syllable and I am faced with a real hopelessness." But here's where I went wrong: "I am sure you feel the same way." And wronger: "After we have been married for a long time, I suppose the problems of communication will be less severe." Maybe George felt the same way, and maybe he didn't; I didn't know then, and I don't know now; but already I'd gotten into the habit of second-guessing his silences. And these would persist, disrupting communication worse than sunspots, for a longer time than I had yet been alive.

How many women have told you, "I thought after we were married he'd come home and we'd have a nice dinner, a little wine, and talk over the day, but instead he walks in and switches on the television and stares until bedtime"? Among women of my age and background, anyway, it's a complaint even more common than chronic fatigue syndrome. We might be willing to listen, but we believe we're supposed to have something to listen *to*: not silence, however companionable. Silence is a symptom, like a pinpoint rash or undulant fever. And every woman is a Florence Nightingale whose task is to make it go away. If you could attend one of our family gatherings, you'd hear just how thoroughly I was trained for this vocation. The din of female voices would daunt any plague of silence threatening to infect our community.

For most men I know, a sudden lull, although it may cause social discomfort, doesn't suggest personal failure as it does for many women, who develop in order to avoid it a variety of conversational strategies that would put any of Jane Austen's characters to shame. Until I rebelled against the prohibitions on sex, religion, and politics and dropped all pretense to polite discourse, my style tended toward what my brother-in-law calls bibble, and I still have an unfortunate fondness for interminable climatic disquisitions. George's mother's style instead takes the form of relentless interrogation. By the time I met him, twenty years of Twenty Questions had drained him of conversational initiative, leaving him terse and, at the first hint of reproach, slightly sullen. He held himself no more responsible for sustaining communication than he was for producing the tunafish sandwich he ate for lunch or retrieving the dirty socks from under his bed.

In many ways George and I made a good match. He was two and a half years older and about four inches taller (the reverse in either case would have been frowned upon). We came from families of European background and similar socioeconomic status, although for Mother's peace of mind he should have been a Congregationalist (and I don't think she knew that his father was a Democrat and his mother an Independent). We went to private colleges, where we both majored in English literature. He preferred Baroque music and I preferred rock and roll, but he liked rock and roll and I liked Baroque music, and we were both crazy about Joan Baez. He was fonder of peanut butter than I but at least he didn't eat liver.

Nobody raised the question of linguistic compatibility. And since we were using roughly the same words in roughly the same order, it hardly seemed likely that my "I do" signified differently from his "I do." Only when my doctoral work led me to read in feminist, psychoanalytic, and linguistic theories did I begin to recognize that, in emotional terms, we'd spent a couple of decades shouting at each other in Urdu and Kikongo without a translator. In practical terms, however, there were few shouts: those still tableaux of my imagination tended to play themselves out in literal, awful silence which, I haltingly came to learn, has a grammar and a rhetoric of its own. What we fear, we are slowest to apprehend, and our stupidity makes us vulnerable.

George felt no fear of silence, and he had a repertoire of uses for it, all of which functioned to augment my anxiety until I became, ironically, speechless. Although he claims that his public silences occur only because he can't think of anything to say, they render him aloof in a manner unnerving even to people who aren't emotionally involved with him. "I always feel like he's judging me," one of our friends once confided, "and I'm not coming off very well." Those of us who are close to him feel his implicit disapproval more strongly. "I'm never scared of you," my daughter told me some years ago with characteristic ego-deflating nonchalance. "You scream and yell but it's nothing. Dad just sits and *looks* and I feel terrible." No matter how benign his attitude, George can't have remained unaware of the power such Olympian silence can confer. He's the least dimwitted man I know.

And not, perhaps, wholly benign. Because I knew from the start (how? how?) that any failings in our relationship rested with me, I could not believe him capable of working us any harm; and so whenever our marriage sputtered and stalled like my old Volvo when the timing went off, I never scrutinized his behavior, only my own. Thus, when we stopped speaking, he could tell me that *I'd* stopped speaking, confident that I wouldn't trace the process back to the moment when, in response to a remark he'd perceived as critical of him, he had shut down absolutely, leaving me too panicked to know what to say. Time after time, I believed that he'd never talk to me again. The marriage was over. It was, each time, the way I imagined drowning to be: soundless but for the shrieks in my fading consciousness.

I've outgrown these anxiety attacks just as I've outgrown agoraphobia. That is, the symptoms still wash over me, and I hate and fear them as much as ever, but I've learned to float face-up until they ebb away again. I suggest to George, whether intentionally or by accident, that his behavior strikes me as flawed. Quiet descends, lasting as a rule no more than a few hours; we don't have days to squander anymore. We'll speak again before we reach the point of divorce. In the meantime, if any crucial information needs to be passed along, we can always tell the dog or the cats, to whom neither of us ever stops speaking, within each other's hearing. In households like ours subject to disruptive lulls, pets are invaluable conduits. People with animal allergies might talk to their plants. Or pray aloud. "Oh God, the toilet has just overflowed and I can't find the plumber's helper. Did you happen to notice where George put it?"

One of the consequences of this susceptibility to silences has been a relationship relatively free of arguments. To the extent—and it's considerable, I think—that this quality has reflected amicability and pleasure in each other's company, it's been a pure blessing. All too often, however, until recent years, it arose from a refusal to risk the discomfort of full engagement. For George, in particular, argument was virtually impossible; he had no siblings to practice with, and his mother dissolves into tears and flees at the first hint of disagreement. Blessed and afflicted with a sister only twenty-one months younger, along with a mother and grandmother who sometimes fought with each other as well as us girls, I had plenty of practice. All the same, the behavior was formally prohibited. Whenever our howls (accompanied on occasion by a bite or a clang on the head with a cast-iron frying pan) escalated to an intolerable din, Sally and I were admonished not to argue rather than instructed how to do it right.

No wonder George and I made a botch of it: I carrying on with the rhetorical extravagance of a girl raised among articulate women, seizing and worrying a subject the way my terrier used to tug and growl at his chew toys; George sneering at my agitation and hyperbole but disdaining to touch the subject at all. "But that's not the point," I'd wail when he accused me of hysteria or exaggeration. "Rhetoric isn't the *point*. Oh, why won't you engage with me?" On May 3, 1985, during a counseling session, he answered: "Because I'm afraid I'll lose." Of course. Why had I been so stupid? Perhaps because I had been raised among women. For me argument had been a means for self-assertion—"giving someone a piece of my mind," we'd called it—rather than a pitched battle which could only result in the "death" of one side or the other. Socialized in the tradition of male ceremonial combat, as Walter J. Ong has called it, George saw me not as a sister or a mother, an other beloved even if at this instant he could cheerfully brain her with the handiest skillet, but as an opponent to be vanquished, and unless he could be sure of "winning," he preferred not to contend at all. By attacking my argumentative style, he diverted attention from the matter between us, and soon we subsided again "safely" into silence.

But, even leaving out our interminable reiteration of these communicative lurches and lapses, was this anything like "marriage" we were saving? In this regard, social and religious attitudes offered little insight, since these focused on the Pageant, which unfolded satisfactorily, on the whole. We produced babies, their genders the wrong way round but one of each, and although we seemed to have married for poorer rather than richer, we made enough money to provide them the elements of a shabby but stable childhood: crumbling houses, second-hand cars, good medical care though no braces for their teeth, library cards, puppies and kitties and bunnies and guinea pigs and some really terrific snakes, back-to-school clothes, a fir tree every Christmas, even a couple of trips to Disneyland. Early on, we sometimes drank too much and smoked a little dope, but we were generally sober, reliable, and polite in company, confining our disagreements behind closed doors. I must have been thirty-five before I got my first, and only, traffic ticket; we weren't arrested for civil disobedience until we were both in our forties.

Of course, there were bad patches—some of them as bad as those potholes in Zaïre capable of swallowing whole trucks, whose roofs become part of the roadbed—but we picked our way across them with as little public fuss as possible. Other people decently averted their eyes whenever they could (as far as I can tell, George's parents got through my six-month sojourn at Met State without breathing a word about it to anyone) or complimented us on our ability to cope with affliction. I don't see how they could have responded otherwise. Pageantry forces an audience into silence and distance.

But as for the Process, spinning out darkly beneath this burnished surface, oh, I was unhappy in it, stricken with grief and guilt for my unhappiness, and unspeakably lonely. I had vowed in front of God and everybody to love and cherish a man of my own choice forever, and I couldn't make good. "I loved this man more than any other person I've ever known," I wept after nine years of marriage. "How could I have stopped? How can I now recoil from his touch? How can he make me feel angry and bitter and bleak instead of full and joyous? Where did it go for God's sake where did it go?" No one had ever suggested to me that "love and cherish" meant "love and cherish on the whole" or "for the most part" or "more often than not" or even "in fits and starts." That much, I found out over the years, I could manage—"the marriage is dead now, of course, but I've lived in it long enough to know that death and resurrection form its characteristic process," I finally realized at about the zillionth such death—but I never believed it was enough, and although I never again had to be locked up, my inconstancy tormented me almost to madness for years to come.

DIS/
RE/
COM/
UNION

W hen I had been married for half my life, the whole rambling, precarious, cockeyed structure George and I had banged together almost toppled down around our ears. The collapse— nothing so definite as a disaster, just a slow sort of dry rot in the posts and beams— really wasn't our fault, I think today. We'd had about as much chance of constructing a shapely and sturdy dwelling place as a couple of blindfolded children turned loose with a heap of toothpicks and marshmallows. Nor was it the fault of anyone else. Calamities are seldom the result of isolable personal shortcomings. They have a genius of their own.

Which is not to say that there weren't good reasons for our marriage to founder. They were endless and excellent. When I think of how poorly couples are prepared for this undertaking, I'm astonished that only one marriage out of two fails. People who wouldn't dream of permitting a child to set off into the wilderness without providing maps and charts, a compass, a Swiss army knife, raingear, sturdy boots, a snake-bite kit, a flashlight, sunscreen, insect repellent, and as many first-hand accounts of previous treks into the territory as they can collect send the same child into marriage with the equivalent of a new pair of tennis shoes and maybe a handful of bandaids. By general standards, George and I weren't all that poorly prepared. The details of the marriages we had known may have been carefully shrouded, but at least the marriages appeared stable and even satisfactory. We knew such an arrangement could be made to work, even if we had no idea how.

Even with more accurate information, however, I suspect our idealism would have blurred our vision, both at the outset and as we went along. "For better or worse," I'd vowed, dutifully parroting the minister's solemn intonation, but I hadn't really meant it. *For better*, I'd meant. *And better. And better.* My prevarication, all unintended, stemmed from the sense of magical immunity which youth and ignorance confer: I knew that some people's marriages got into trouble, but I didn't believe that ours could ever make us unhappy—at least nowhere near as unhappy as it eventually proved capable of making us. We believed ourselves exceptional, just as every other bride and groom do when they publicly pledge themselves "for better," "for richer," "in health," secretly leaving the "worse" and "poorer" and "sickness" for some other, unexceptional couple.

Ready or not, George and I were married just as a social

upheaval was beginning to call traditional institutions of all kinds, not merely matrimony, into question. Quickly, "doing your own thing" assumed a kind of moral force, making it possible for me to write a decade after our wedding: "George and I now know that we may not be married forever—that we are committed to personal growth, which necessarily involves the risk of growing apart." It doesn't necessarily involve any such thing, but an alternative model—a model in which the commitment might be to generating and sustaining an indissoluble relationship, from which personal growth would result, if not necessarily, then at least probably, simply because so difficult a task tends to force development—was hard to conceive during the heady self-celebration of the sixties and seventies.

Acting on the premise of personal growth (inasmuch as I can be said to have acted on anything so rational as a premise), I permitted myself from quite early on to have extramarital affairs: infrequent, short-lived, noncommittal, generally discreet. And passionate. That's what I loved about them, their capacity for waking me from the torpor into which my spirits habitually sank to such terrifying depths that I couldn't tell whether I was dead or alive. I was neither, I know now, but floating in the half-drowned state of clinical depression, and if I had been medicated consistently, I might never have needed these rough rousings. Can biochemistry legitimately be held responsible for sin? Can psychopharmacology be employed to prevent it?

Not that I thought of these affairs as sins. "Sin" is not a very seventies word. I'd have been mortally embarrassed to admit it into my thoughts, much less my conversation. I don't think I actually condoned my adulteries. Sometimes I even dreaded them. But I believed myself powerless to resist them: "Goddamn men for their largess with trivial attentions," I wrote at the first signs of one that blessedly failed to materialize. "They're like stupid zookeepers who casually saunter into the cages of sleeping tigers; and when the creatures stir and growl, they say, 'Go to sleep again, good pussies.' Don't they understand that an aroused beast does not go back to sleep—it rages?" Patristic texts at their most virulent do not surpass the misogyny underlying this image: I, the trapped feral animal, all sleekness and grace and fury, carelessly kept by the man who should guard and tame me.

No wonder I was morally vacuous. Tigers do not by any stretch of the imagination fret over their possible or actual trespasses. They just do what comes naturally. Even years later, well after my conversion to Catholicism, as I was contemplating whether or not to begin what would turn out to be my last affair, I didn't employ moral terms: "Having an affair requires a lot of effort, a lot of attention to another person. Sometimes I feel like bothering, but often as not I don't." The ghost of the tiger lingers, lolling in the shade, amber eyes slitted sleepily as she watches the heedless man and sniffs his tantalizing scent. He's not awfully plump, but she's a little hungry. Is he worth the effort of eating?

Fidelity, I had begun to think after the first hectic conjugal flush had faded, condemned me to a life of self-deprivation. That it offered me a means for self-discipline never crossed my mind. "Discipline" had only cheerless connotations: parental spankings, after-school detention, parking tickets, all measures to make of me a more compliant person than I was sure I cared to be. To the extent that it entailed choice, it obliged me to take the most distasteful option available: cramming for a biology exam when I felt like writing a poem, going without a new dress in order to pay the telephone bill. I never associated it with satisfaction, certainly not with joy, and its relation to personal growth entirely escaped me for nearly twenty years.

I'd like to claim that a flash of moral illumination put an end to my infidelities, but I can't even do that. I simply lost interest in men in that way. Perhaps the highs and lows wore me out. Or perhaps I'm only suffering from sour grapes, since within a few years I'd grown too old and crippled to interest men in that way. Certainly it's more than coincidence that my depression was brought under medical control at about the same time. But no, gradually I've come to discern a genuine moral dimension to my changed attitude. I lost interest in men because I began to assume responsibility for rousing myself: not a somnolent tiger, not a beast at all, but a woman, a writing woman, a woman inscribing a life. Such a process necessitates moral choice. I'd been choosing all along, of course, but obliviously; now I had to attend to what I was doing.

Now I was capable of sin. If only I could figure out what sin was. This task ought to be simpler than I've found it. I don't mean I had trouble discovering what deeds are deemed sinful; no student of literature with a special interest in Old and Middle English can help but have the Seven Deadlies inscribed on her brain. Nor was the sinner's fate in doubt: *"In this life sinners suffer* from remorse of conscience, fear, and unhappiness. Their *sin often brings* upon them *disease* or *death*, the *hatred* and *scorn* of their fellow-men, and other temporal punishments," says one particularly lurid religious manual, and after death "the unrepentant sinner is punished in *hell*."[1] But the truth is that I've known all kinds of furious, greedy, lustful, jealous, slothful, gluttonous, vainglorious people (though seldom all at once) who were clearly having a whale of a time. My own adulteries didn't make me wholly miserable; to be honest, I had some lovely interludes. If I believed in hell, perhaps I could take some satisfaction in believing that they'd get theirs, and I mine; but on the matter of hell I remain on the skeptical side of agnostic.

Yet I now believe that adultery is a sin and that sin is retroactive—that is, that whatever I've done is no less wicked simply because I didn't perceive it in that light at the time. In part through reading and reflecting upon Christian teachings from the Gospels onward, but also through the very experiences I now renounce, I have come to apprehend sin as the state into which I'm thrown whenever I choose, consciously or not, to act in a manner that frays or severs the bonds of love between me and my fellow creatures, between me and the God present to me through those creatures. Viewed in this way, in terms of conditions and consequences, no deed can be judged sinful outside of its context, and the definition of a deed's sinfulness can be disconcertingly ambiguous. If you take pride in your child's performance as a Thanksgiving turkey in the school play, for example, your delight and praise will strengthen her for the next challenge, and even open boasting, though it may bore your friends, is no sin. But if you treat her badly—make her mop up a glass of milk you later discover she didn't spill, say, or refer to the first boy she ever loves as a mooncalf—and are too prideful to apologize to her, your offense is great. Transgression consists not in breaking an inflexible rule against Pride but in disrupting mutual affection.

I married for love—most everybody does these days—and when I pledged, in the course of the Christian marriage ceremony, to forsake all others so long as George and I both lived, I affirmed marital affection to be not merely mutual but exclusive and perdurable, qualities annulled by adultery. Although legally I could unspeak my vows at any time, thereby altering the context of my actions, a web of other forces—largely social and financial to begin with but over time spiritual as well—permitted me to transgress but not to dissolve the conjugal bond. I couldn't shake the sense that marriage was something more than an economic contract between two men, the father who bestows and the husband who receives the bartered bride, and that, although the practical benefit of fidelity is to ensure the legitimacy of the husband's offspring, it holds a symbolic value as well: the gift of self, freely and lovingly dispensed as a sign of abiding commitment. Violating my vows did not absolve me of them, I felt sure, as long as I persisted in believing that what God joins, no one—not even I at my wickedest—may put asunder.

Nevertheless, I was free to violate them if I wished. Sin is always an option. As is its opposite. One of the splendid features of the liturgical year is that the same stories come round again and again, at least once every three years; if you go to church over a long enough span, you get second and seventh and twentieth chances to tease out their meanings, which multiply as your experience deepens. Jesus did not condemn the woman caught in adultery, and far from punishing her, he protected her from punishment. "Go," he said to her then, "and do not sin again." Clearly, I recognized after who knows how many readings, he believed her capable of choosing this course of action without being threatened and of carrying out her choice. Being a faithful wife meant more than denying myself the giddy rush brought on by a new lover in order to preserve myself from hellfire I didn't even believe in. It meant choosing George over and over and over: a lifetime of weddings.

With the irony only real life permits, just as I gave up trying to escape marriage and started to settle into it as into a rambling old house, the kind one knows will demand a lifetime in restoration and upkeep but promises to be so graceful and commodious, with its waxed pine floorboards and tall windows and deep veranda draped with wisteria, that no amount of work will seem wasted, George decided to leave. "I've always believed that we'd grow old together," I mourned when he told me, "that he'd make the trip toward death with me and that we'd make that particular hard journey easier for each other. Now he's getting off at a way station. Now he's getting off." We'd been married nineteen years. "But George has never been good at initiating action—tends to wait for a push from me," I observed as he teetered for months on the threshold. "Is it my job now to push him out of my life, whether I want him to go or not, for his own good? I don't want to be without him, but neither can I stand to hold him here with me for my own comfort and protection, knowing that I make him miserable and that he's here only because he's too weak and too kind—a tricky combination—to make a drastic change."

The months turned into years: 1982, 1983, 1984. . . . And because he did not ever physically depart—return to New England to find a teaching job and another woman as he contemplated—George believed that he'd stayed after all. But he went, I assure you, he set off alone into some remote and inaccessible landscape, leaving behind a golem whose hollow presence fooled the eyes of strangers, and maybe even most friends, but tormented me in ways that outright separation might not have done. The golem was not in love with me. When I returned from an out-of-town reading, it told me it didn't care one way or the other, didn't miss me while I was gone, wasn't glad when I came back. Taking a second job, it stayed away from the house long hours; when there, it pottered silently, laying tiles in the bathroom, repairing light fixtures, watering plants. At night, instead of making love to me, it scooted to the edge of the bed and clung there like a limpet. "I'm comfortable with myself," it told me when I suggested counseling, "and don't feel any need to change."

I felt the need, all right, but not the capacity: "I can't 'win him back.' I am, after all, the same person who lost him in the first place. I can't get rid of the things that make me me—my crippledness, my writing, this slow deep steady feeling for George that he would not call love. It's *this* woman that he doesn't love. *This* woman is *me*." If my faithlessness, now at an end, had worn him out, he never told me so. He was not in the habit of explaining himself. Left to my own devices, I experienced the central issue as a kind of vocational conflict: "*This* woman" could be either an attentive wife or a committed writer but not both, because whenever I became absorbed in my work, he found me cold and remote. "What a bind," I noted cheerlessly. "I don't see how I could survive, let alone work, without him—but when I feel safe with him and thus free to work, I start, through my preoccupation, to lose him." In the gamble of my life, I chose work.

At the heart of this dilemma—a false one, to be sure, but perfectly real—was feminism: "It's that wicked feminism which has stolen away his helpless, guilt-ridden wife who couldn't always perhaps see things in his accurate way but who always *tried*, at least, and now she's not even trying, she's just balky and stubborn, truly perverse, truly a witch. . . . He's got to have something to blame. The possibility that he's simply been an awful shit—quite unconsciously—all his life is inadmissable. The problem is all in my poor little mind, contaminated now by feminism." This passage, written at my bitterest, caricatures George's response, but in truth he did hold feminism, rather than the extramarital affair in which he was by this time deeply involved, responsible for our marital difficulties. If I'd found out about his infidelity, he'd likely have laid that at my feminist feet, too. He has not been an awful shit all his life, or even very much of it, but here and there he's outdone himself.

His choice of scapegoat seems especially ironic now. But not wholly inaccurate. "Ever since you found feminism," he accused, "you act as though you're on some higher level." Feminism never provided me quite the aura of religious enlightenment suggested by "found"; and "higher" reflects his own anxieties about dominance; but my sense of locus did shift, though outward rather than upward, as I scrutinized my life for the assumptions on which it was based and questioned how I'd come to collaborate in those assumptions. It was this shift that George hated, I think, because it inevitably undermined his own stance. You really can discount the person at the other end of the seesaw as a cold and crazy bitch or any other damned thing you please only so long as she stays in place, but if she dismounts and wanders away, you're left sitting on the ground with your jaw hanging. George scrabbled to his feet and fled.

For me, feminism had several practical consequences— among them directing a project in women's studies, finishing my Ph.D., winning a major poetry award, publishing a book of poems and a book of essays, securing several good job offers and later a sizable advance on a new book—but fleeing was not one of them. On the contrary, even when I decided to teach at UCLA while George remained in Tucson until Matthew graduated from high school, I stated clearly that I considered the arrangement financially necessary but temporary, a "commuter marriage" that would end as quickly as feasible in our reunion. "I guess I've given up on us," George had told me not long before. "I just assume we're going our different ways." "Do you ever say, 'I'm going my different way,'" I asked, "or is it always 'We're going our different ways'?" but he was so used to defining the world for both of us that he didn't get the distinction. I couldn't help that. He could go his different way if he had to, but I wasn't going anywhere. Not in the way he meant.

In spite of all these emotional comings and goings, we never actually parted, and I've often wondered why not. My favorite private theory is that we're permanently bonded because we smell right to each other, joined in olfactory wedlock, so to speak, but people generally look shocked when I mention it, there's something so primordial about sniffing each other out, so I guess I should come up with a public theory a little less baldly corporeal. Certainly for years our poverty pressed us to remain together; we could scarcely keep one household afloat, let alone provide adequately for two. Much of the time, an even more powerful factor has been social, and especially familial, expectation. Divorce has not been common in either of our families or among our closest friends. We're Yankees at heart, good Puritan stock, people of our word, hardy and severe: "You've made your bed," we say, "now lie in it." Divorce signifies failure: of love, of course, but also of will. We're too proud for it.

Had we been Catholics from the outset, we might have considered ourselves stuck with each other—body odor, scanty resources, and propriety notwithstanding—since one of the essential properties of marriage defined by canon law is indissolubility. As with virtually every other pronouncement of the Church, I'm of several minds about the intent and implications of this. I have never doubted, before or after becoming a Catholic, that my marriage to George had permanent force. I'd vowed as much in perfectly plain language—"till death us do part"— and a woman must be taken at her word. To the extent that the Church intends to support and strengthen me in fulfilling that vow, I'm grateful for the help. I can use all the help I can get.

But in effect, the Church's stand seems more coercive and punitive than supportive. The prohibition of sexual relationships between single people precipitates risky marriages. The denial of remarriage to divorced Catholics excludes them from a supportive community they may most need. Annulment, which is increasingly easy to obtain, puts people in the emotionally and morally dubious position of avowing that their marriage was never valid in the first place. In bitterness, many may believe this; but for spiritual health, they need to be encouraged to value, not despise, their human connections, to let them go when necessary without repudiating them, and to form new ones with fresh wisdom and care. The Church's inflexibility doesn't prevent divorce and remarriage; it simply drives those who choose them away.

The ones who remain have traditionally been offered a model of matrimony worse than useless. "Every couple should imitate the peace and love that reigned in the home of the Blessed Virgin and St. Joseph, the models of Christian spouses," one manual admonishes.[2] Oh, come on. Who knows what went on behind the mud walls of that carpenter's house in Nazareth? What help does an empty model provide two people for whom the preservation of civility and even sanity is a livelier goal than sainthood any day? In recent years, a less treacly and more pragmatic view of marriage may have emerged, at least among progressive Catholics. Premarital instruction is mandated, and retreats like Engaged Encounter offer couples the opportunity to reflect on their commitment and explore their expectations. Celibate clergy still advise couples on matters they're required never to experience, but at least they are often trained in counseling.

The fact remains, however, that the Church takes its very identity from a marital model based on domination and subordination: Christ is the Bridegroom; the Church, the Bride; and there's no mistaking who's in charge of whom. "Husbands, love your wives, as Christ loved the church," the Letter to the Ephesians exhorts; "Wives, be subject to your husbands, as to the Lord. For the husband is the head of the wife. . . ." (Eph. 5.25,22) Now this isn't as bad as it sounds, says the pope, because "in marriage there is mutual 'subjection of the spouses out of reverence for Christ', and not just that of the wife to the husband"; moreover, "*all human beings—both women and men—are called* through the Church, *to be the 'Bride' of Christ. . . . In this way 'being the bride', and thus the 'feminine' element, becomes a symbol of all that is 'human'. . . ."* [3]

Listen, guys, you can take it from me, being a woman in our society, even a purely symbolic one, is not all that hot, and any spousal relationship, whether human or divine, which is structured in terms of "heads" and "subjects" violates the radical mutuality of realized love, both ours for one another and Christ's for us. Better we should drop the wedding imagery altogether, corrupted as it is by centuries of inequity, and think of ourselves in terms of identity: not the Bride but the Body of Christ. We enact Christ. Through us Christ enters the world. Christ needs us in order to become present even as we need Christ to give our enactment of that presence significance. This is real love we're talking about, passionate, reciprocal, incarnate. In a church modeled on such love, matrimony becomes truly holy.

Whether this Church will become that church remains to be seen. If it can transform itself from an exclusive to an inclusive institution, one that views all its participants equally as very members incorporate in the mystical body of Christ, to use the beautiful language of *The Book of Common Prayer*, new paradigms of partnership, both homosexual and heterosexual, will evolve intermediate between indissoluble marriage and perpetual celibacy. I especially like one proposed by the controversial Episcopal bishop John Shelby Sprong, which provides for the formal betrothal of two people who are certain of the seriousness of their relationship but not of its permanence, freeing them of both sexual guilt and the stigma (though not perhaps the pain) of divorce. Marriage would be reserved for those willing to make a lifelong commitment, especially those wishing to bear and raise children.

The bonds of such a marriage are best thought of as indissoluble so that we'll give them time to work. Otherwise, in a society that throws away diapers after the first soiling instead of dealing with an infant's shit, at the first twinge of conflict or boredom marriage would get sent to the nearest spiritual landfill. But life is very long, and getting longer; and a marriage contracted in one's twenties may no longer be a marriage a couple of decades later. In that case, dissolution has already taken place, Church sanctions be damned, and new arrangements must be worked out without the blame that so often strikes people as an inevitable, even a necessary response when, really, rarely are the actions of individuals reprehensible. We all want to be good to one another, and if we can't manage it under some conditions, perhaps new ones will be more enabling. But surely ascribing blame and taking sides are always disabling.

"Do you believe that you are marrying Eric forever?" I asked my daughter, about six months before her wedding, when she came in during these meditations and plumped down on the shabby sofa across from me.

"Yes!" she said in her of-course-Mother-how-can-you-be-so-dimwitted-as-to-ask? voice. But I do have to ask. She's a whole generation away from me, and of a more pragmatic nature. I'm sure she doesn't think of marriage in terms of a "vocation" or "spiritual discipline," concepts she probably considers pretty goofy. I can see clearly that she has a moral life, but I'm not certain how marriage fits into it. She might have said "as long as it's good for us" or "we'll take it one day at a time"—not bad aspirations but not, I would argue, *enough*. Only forever is enough.

"Oh, good," I said. "I've been writing down my thoughts about marriage," I went on, sheepishly, "and they're . . . conservative." This made her laugh; she and Eric are our resident conservatives. "But I don't see how you can get anywhere, spiritually speaking, if you keep turning in one marriage on another like used cars." She nodded, perhaps remembering how, just a year before, sitting in this little room, I'd told her about her father's infidelity and my determination not to turn the marriage in, perhaps basking in the diffuse joy generated by that decision. She even permitted me "spiritually." I could hardly wait for the wedding.

"Marriage requires the continual breaking of ground, going where one has never gone before," I reflected in 1982 when George first mentioned leaving me. "First marriages, anyway, and second ones that last longer than the first. I hear George saying that he wants to move back, not forward, to go home where it's safe, to do again what he's sure he can do. I wonder if his desire comes out of a fear of death. If he goes on, he has to move closer to dying. If he circles round and starts over, then he's twenty again, not forty. Whatever the cause, I'm helpless in the face of his longing. With me there's no starting over, only going on. I'm aging, fading, before his eyes. With me he can only travel toward death." To go on, and on, and on, God knows where, to have the whole adventure: holy matrimony.

"I, Nancy, take you, George. . . . " I had intended to speak firmly this time, but my voice is whispery and tremulous again. Outside the wide window of the little chapel at the Desert House of Prayer, the landscape trembles, pale and dry already in the mid-May heat, so different from wet, wind-tossed maples against a slaty sky that we could never have dreamed it a quarter of a century ago. In place of white taffeta, I'm dressed in heavy cotton knit, cream and tan; George wears not a morning coat but a rose-colored shirt with stripes of cream and blue, a graying beard, glasses. Within a small semicircle of close relatives and friends, we stand with Father Ricardo and make anew all those promises it's a good thing we didn't understand the significance of the first time around. "Poorer" didn't turn out to be so bad, but "worse" has sometimes been dreadful indeed, "sickness" meant cancer and multiple sclerosis, and "death" really will part us, perhaps before very long. The ignorance that protected those children, waifish in their dress-up clothes, smiling, stunned—the ones we always laugh at in the wedding album, exclaiming, "Who'd let two babies like that get married?"—has worn away. We know now. We promise anyway.

Twenty-five years is probably just about the right length of time for a courtship, and I really do feel I'm marrying George in a new way. For one thing, I'm not sick with dread this time. Weddings in our society seem designed to reduce the bride and groom to precisely the condition of those who, because they "lack sufficient use of reason," are "incapable of contracting marriage," according to canon law. What with the gown to be chosen and fitted (smaller and smaller as the strain takes its toll), the color scheme settled on, the attendants' attire selected, the hall hired, the caterer and photographer booked, the flowers ordered, the china and silver and crystal patterns registered, the invitations printed and mailed, the gifts opened and acknowledged (the sixth pair of salt and pepper shakers just as rapturously as the first), the ceremony rehearsed, and the guests assembled, all eyes trained on the happy couple, who are obligated to turn in a perfect performance on this most momentous occasion of their entire lives, it's no wonder if their voices tremble less with joy than with exhaustion and stage fright. I knew I was supposed to look radiant and greet each guest graciously, even the ones I'd never laid eyes on before. No one ever mentioned having a good time. The most telling photographs in our wedding album are the ones in which George and I wear not revelers' grins but the stares of deer caught in the headlights of an onrushing automobile.

After a full day of celebrating their fiftieth anniversary, George's parents exclaimed how much more fun they'd had than at their wedding, and now we know what they meant. Except for a couple of brief conversations with a caterer whose work we already knew and a morning's maddening search for suitable cocktail plates and napkins that weren't all gooped up with silver bows and bells, we've hardly fussed at all. I bought my dress on impulse, with no particular occasion in mind, from a sale rack in a shop going bankrupt. Friends sent us a stunning bouquet of two dozen salmon-colored roses or we'd have no flowers. I woke feeling excited, not nervous (the physical sensations of these two states are almost indistinguishable, but you'll like them better if you call them "excitement"). The tremor in my voice as I pledge to cherish George forever betrays neither fatigue nor fear but the intense thrill of renewal.

This time we exchange our vows as Catholics. Not that the first ones didn't count, even in the eyes of the Church, because of course they did. But they were largely social rather than sacramental in nature, entitling George and me to use the same last name, live openly together, have sexual intercourse whenever we wanted, bear children legitimately, carry them and each other on our health insurance policies, and inherit jointly owned property without putting it through probate when one of us died, all the while enjoying the community's approbation so long as we didn't go too deeply into debt, let our house and yard deteriorate into an eyesore, or scream at each other in public. Viewing ourselves as responsible primarily for each other's spiritual well-being, and then for the spiritual well-being of the world, would have struck me as a ludicrous piety.

Insofar as I involved God in making and carrying out those first vows, he was the Daddy God, pleasing whom entailed a list of onerous prescriptions and prohibitions. The fact that these took their most basic form as commandments suggested that human nature had to be forced into goodness; left to its own devices, it would prefer idols, profanity, leisurely Sunday mornings with bagels and the *New York Times*, disrespect for authority, murder, adultery, theft, lies, and everything belonging to the guy next door. I'm questioning here not these strictures themselves, most of which I accept at face value, but the view of the human creature underlying their form. In it, I was forever on the perilous verge of doing a don't, to atone for which I had to beg forgiveness from the very being who had set me up for trespass, by forbidding behaviors he clearly expected me to commit, in the first place: the God of the Gotcha, you might say. It's awfully hard to achieve spiritual health in relation to a being who appears eager to condemn you so that he can then magnanimously redeem you from your own nasty nature. His power corrupts the bond between you. It's far easier to thrive in the care of one who, thrilled with the goodness of her whole creation, asks for the single act that will make transgression impossible: love.

Oh, how I quail at using that word! It's been so sentimentalized in contemporary culture that almost all its resonances have been smothered in a drift of red hearts and teddy bears: I ♥ NY. I ♥ MY VOLVO. JESUS ♥ YOU. It's a transitive verb whose object is always pleasing; the instant the object ceases to delight, we switch the verb to "like" or "can live without" or "downright detest." But the great commandment permits no lexical shift. The only verb is "love," and the objects it takes are designated without regard to your pleasure: (1) God; (2) everybody else, yourself included. If you love God with all your heart and all your soul and all your mind and also love your neighbor as yourself, you will naturally carry out all the other commandments as well. Of course, this is a harder task than any they set. I've had far less trouble refraining from adultery, in the years since I discovered I had the power to choose fidelity, than I've had loving Ronald Reagan, for instance; in fact, I've never quite accomplished the latter.

Conceiving love only as a warm fuzzy, you can readily forget just how much work it entails. But it's authentic work, strenuous and productive: doing a do, not avoiding a don't. It puts you in a right relation with God and others, reciprocal rather than hierarchical. At one time or another, legal penalties have been imposed for violations of all the ten commandments, and still are for some (a "stubborn child" may still be turned over to the state in Massachusetts, for example). But the great commandment is extralegal. Love cannot be forced. It must be chosen. You love not out of dread but out of your own fullness. It's what you were made for. When you fail at it, you aren't sent to prison, or to the electric chair, or to hell. You are commanded again: Love.

By the time I make my marital vows to George for the second time, I believe myself capable of this kind of love: mutual and without condition. As usual, overestimating my spiritual stamina, I'm a little bit right and a little bit wrong—but righter, in this case, than wrong, as I will prove a couple of years after this celebration when I learn of his infidelity. I can indeed love George, more often than not, in a way that reflects the love of God. The terms of our first marriage—social propriety, sexual and intellectual compatibility, personal growth, responsibility for our children—were sound and honorable enough, but they failed to yield metaphors that would transcend the mechanical and legalistic elements of our union. For this we need to set our vows within the Mass, which incarnates love.

"The Body of Christ," George says, placing the wafer on my tongue. The words both describe this scrap of bread and affirm my identity: a double mystery. I eat the Body of Christ. I am—we are all—the Body of Christ. Nourished by God, we must bear God into the world and give God away with ourselves.

As Philip Slater long since pointed out, we are a society of hoarders, not just materially but also spiritually, organizing our attitudes and activities on the premise that there's never enough of anything to go around.[4] Among the myriad and complex consequences of structuring our lives in terms of scarcity rather than abundance is the sense of the self as a depletable resource in danger of trickling away like the dried beans that leaked from my son's childhood pig Wilbur, leaving only a limp rag of purple plush. The self-husbandry such a concept necessitates—the drive for "personal growth" in the sense of "individual growth"—starves any relationship, but especially as energy-intensive a relationship as marriage. Marriage requires a sense of the self not as the tumescent male who fears that, after ejaculation, his penis will wilt and droop, never to rise and spurt again, but as the nursing mother who knows that the more voraciously her infant sucks, the more milk her breasts will produce.

"The Blood of Christ," I say to George, and he takes the pottery chalice and drinks. The Eucharist is inexhaustible, we feed on it week after week, and in configuring our relationship to reflect it, George and I nourish and sustain each other. Instead of eating each other up, we find we have enough, more than we'd ever dreamed, a surplus, a superabundance, plenty to squander in every direction and more where that came from, so much that we even lavish it on our poor foolish corgi, who sighs and rolls his eyes as George scrubs the remains from the yogurt carton off his nose, and the hummingbirds who, hovering around the empty feeder, peer through the back window and screech "juice! juice!" and one day—why not?—even worms, even daisies.

ROOM
FOR
ONE MORE

❦

One Saturday morning several years ago, when my mother and I were talking on the telephone as we do every week, she expressed regret at living on the other side of the country from my sister's girls. At that time my foster son, Ron, had returned with his family to Iceland for a second tour of duty, and so I commiserated with Mother. In our highly mobile society, grandmothering is apt to take place in crude stop-motion: the lisping toddler in droopy diapers who gives you a milky kiss as he leaves your front door shows up at it next as a blur in bluejeans with the pockets full of marbles, his lips sticky under a red Kool-Aid moustache, and then maybe as a skate punk in RayBans and neon-bright jams, even his hair defying gravity. . . .

"Oh," Mother said when I referred wistfully to Ron's boys, Alex and C.J., "but those aren't your *real* grandchildren." I wasn't so sure about that. They'd seemed real enough to me on their last visit to Cactus Grandma and Cactus Grandpa, as they call us, their solid sweaty little-boy bodies electric with energy. But of course the reality Mother was calling into question had to do not with their substance, which she had seen for herself, but with their entitlement to a particular claim upon me (and thus, at another remove, upon herself). Her point was that the boys and I shared no genetic material. Being related "by blood," this sharing is called, though since every cell has DNA one might just as well say "by snot," which would go a long way toward demystifying an essentially troublesome distinction.

"Blood is thicker than water," the adage goes, reflecting the primacy traditionally accorded to familial bonds by basing them not on mere proximity, an assortment of bodies gathered under one roof, but on consanguinity, the blood flowing through those bodies held in common. In these terms, I am connected to my own children more closely than I am not only to Ron and his sons but also to my children's father. The children and I don't literally share our blood, of course. During the brief period when we did, thanks to the presence of a factor in their blood which is absent in mine, we proved so incompatible that now a transfusion of anybody's blood but my own would cause mine to "clump," a sort of blood-is-thicker-than-blood condition that I'm told would be very bad for me indeed. So we keep our precious bodily fluids to ourselves. All the same, I do feel connections with them I don't feel with anyone else, the essence of which I can't firmly identify.

I conceived Anne on Christmas Eve 1964, as I did just about

everything else when I was twenty-one, because I was supposed to. I had been married a decent interval, which for Catholics might be nine months to the day from the wedding night but for Protestants was a little longer so as to demonstrate our enlightened use of birth control, and now a baby was expected of me. I wasn't at all reluctant, mind you, since my fulfillment depended on this step. In the same way that no woman who could find a husband would choose to remain a "spinster," no woman who could get pregnant would choose to remain childless. A woman who couldn't get pregnant could always adopt an infant (Catholic infants for Catholics and Protestant ones for Protestants, so that a blue-eyed, straw-haired family like mine didn't wind up with a baby whose wide black gaze and dark ringlets marked her outsider status), but adoption was second-best and the woman who had to settle for it was not only pitied but ever-so-slightly scorned because she "couldn't have" children. (Since her husband's sperm count was never mentioned, the deficiency was at least tacitly ascribed to her.) So I was relieved when my pregnancy was confirmed. Marriage had let me down a bit, but this time I was definitely on my way to fulfillment.

The funny thing is that I really was on my way, but the route was so circuitous and the fulfillment so different from anything I'd been led to expect that I spent years in a panic, certain I'd taken one wrong turn after another, certain I was irredeemably lost in the Black Bog of Bad Motherhood. I suspect now that other women were stumbling and sloshing through the same terrain, but the Bog's distinctive feature is a miasma so thick that nothing—not a footfall, not a groan or whimper—penetrates it. One is only alone there. As far as I could tell, every other woman was managing motherhood as though she were born to it; and so closely did I control my terror and chagrin most of the time that every other woman may have thought that I was doing the same.

Anne was born, and remained, a golden girl: smart, funny, self-possessed, the kind who talks whole sentences at a year and learns to read in nursery school and sails straight on to become a National Merit Scholar, graduate from Smith *magna cum laude*, join the Peace Corps, enter graduate school, marry the man you'd have chosen if arranged marriages were still in vogue. . . . At about the time she was exiting her teens, I asked her how come she'd never rebelled, and she shrugged: "I guess I never saw any need to." True enough. From birth, she'd done as she damned well pleased; luckily for her, what pleased her to do pleased the rest of us as well. Even a child this easy proved too much for me, however, and when she was two I turned her over to my mother for the six months I spent in a mental hospital. Although the reasons for my breakdown were complicated, as I've suggested here and elsewhere, at the time I perceived them to coalesce around my inability to take care of—or even to "want"—my own child.

Nonetheless, pressured again by social expectations and also by George, himself an only child, I was determined to have another baby. But because of our Rh incompatibility, Matthew was born jaundiced. Snatched from my vagina, given an exchange of blood, and deposited in an isolette, he was a week old before I was allowed to touch him, and whatever bonding might have taken place at birth was aborted. We have spent the rest of our lives trying to recover from this trauma. Once, when I asked an elderly friend if she regretted not having had children, she responded in her characteristically forthright manner: "It was the great tragedy of my life." Each life must hold one, I think: one pain that overarches and obscures all others, one haunting irreversible fault for which one can never atone. Matthew's botched birth constitutes my great tragedy.

From the outset he cried through most of his waking hours, all the more fiercely if I held and cuddled him; grief-stricken at his rejection, I retreated into the role of caretaker, dutiful enough but distant and wary. For years, I believed that I didn't love him: "He was the most heart-breakingly beautiful baby I've ever seen," I reflected in my journal, "and I rejected him wholly. . . . This must be the bitterest thing that can happen to a woman, to be deprived of her own child in this way—worse than death, because then one can go on loving the lost child—a kind of death in life, to have the child but not the love." I felt certain that he knew of my failure and despised me for it: "I'm so ashamed in the face of his knowledge that I can hardly bear to be with him. I wonder if there'll ever come a time when he can understand my grief, forgive me even. No, why should he?"

As he entered the tumultuous and defiant adolescence Anne had never seen a need for, I could scarcely stand the sight of him, "both sides of his head shaved, the hair on top sticking up in clumps. Neck and arms draped with chains and padlocks, studded strips of leather, filthy camouflage bandannas, loud neckties. His clothing from Value Village (cheap, at least), ill-fitting, the colors clashing." According to the "imaginary-ideal-Matthew" theory his father and his grandparents subscribed to, "inside this hideous exterior is a heart of gold, a fine upstanding young man, a brilliant student, impeccably dressed and aesthetically refined, if only one could find the key to set him free. I don't subscribe. There's only one Matthew. What you see is what you get. So let him be."

Only gradually did it occur to me that these complicated responses—grief at the other's rejection, terror for the other's well-being and guilt for endangering it, attention to the minutest aspects of the other's condition, defense of the other's right to choose his own way—are the marks not of repulsion but of passionate attachment. Everything in my experience and education had suggested that "love" was reactive, an upwelling of delight caused by the beloved's pleasing looks or ways. My beloved did not please me. In fact, much of the time he drove me stark ravers. But he absorbed me utterly. And still does. Just this morning we were playing computers, a sport that highlights not only the quickness and grace of his mind but also his tact as a teacher. I'm installing a new system and turning my old one over to him, a process that would render me paralytic with stupidity if he didn't keep reassuring me that what we're having here is *fun*. Now he's gone off, and my studio, which generally looks as though a whirlwind had recently torn through, has achieved a new apotheosis of chaos, crowned by his forgotten black felt hat on top of the bookcase. We're just like that, Matthew and I.

If *this* is love—and it is—then I can faintly glimpse what the love of God might be. So long as I understood it as a response to my pleasingness—*if* I was good, *then* God would love me (and contrariwise, if I was bad, then God would throw me into hell, the most hateful gesture imaginable)—I couldn't believe in it, since the chances of my ever being good enough to merit the love of God were slenderer than a strand of silk. But suppose God takes no particular delight in me at all. Suppose God finds me about as attractive as I found Matthew during the years when razorblades dangled from his ears and his room was littered with plates and glasses growing long green hairs and his favorite band was called Useless Pieces of Shit. Suppose God keeps me steadily in sight, agonizing over my drunken motorcycle rides and failed courses, laughing at my jokes, putting in earplugs and attending my gigs, signing for my release at the police station, weeping with me as we bury the dead dog. . . . Oh, I feel certain that she does.

Still, I'm not God, or anything like. I'm only a mother, and possibly a bad one at that. At least, I was told so often enough. I never seemed to get anything right. When I returned to work a year after Matthew's birth, my mother accused me of deserting her grandchildren, and although she now acknowledges that it seems to have done them no harm, I was haunted throughout their childhood by the conviction that my professional life, which I believed I needed not just for the money but for my sanity, rendered me neglectful and selfish. By the time, fifteen years later, George's father condemned me for failing to make Matthew get a decent haircut and decent clothes and decent friends (clothes making the man and a man being known by the company he keeps), I was no longer willing to take the blame any more than I accepted praise for Anne's accomplishments. But I could have used a little praise for my own accomplishments: In the couple of decades that I had at least one child in the house, no one ever exclaimed, "Gee, Nancy, that was a nifty bit of mothering there!"

George least of all. He shared in the childcare from the outset, even changing "dirty" diapers (this always seemed to be held up as the mark of paternal devotion, that a man would muck about with his baby's shit), and his involvement excited admiration, at least from other women, especially me. No one would have said of me that I shared in the childcare, much less admired my generosity in sparing George some of the work. This was the sixties, and the lot fell to me. In fathering children, a man produced "mouths to feed," but the obligation was metaphorical: George had to make enough money to procure the strained peas, but no one expected him to pop the lid off the jar, spoon the glop into a rosebud mouth, and then block the spray before the kitchen took on the hue of the Owl and the Pussycat's boat. Nor was I admired for sharing in the task of pea-procurement. What was sauce for the gander was in those days definitely not sauce for the goose.

I am only pointing out the imbalance in gender expectations here, not denigrating George's participation in childrearing. He was an exceptional caregiver, attentive, companionable, humorous, at times unquestionably a better mother to the children than I, especially during the period when I really did abandon them, sinking into depression, moving out of the house, and attempting suicide. Ironically, however, this depression may have been triggered by his increasing remoteness, for as the children grew older he began to pull away from us all. Far from sharing in the childcare, now that the care entailed not bedtime baths and goofy games but sexual guidance, supervision of homework and chores, disciplinary action, he devoted all his energy to pea-procurement, not just for us but for the needy world beyond our door, and after a while, in secret, to Sandra, who sent her child away before he ever got there, providing him a tidy, tranquil refuge. Every family with adolescents must have a resident Big Meany, and he wasn't about to be It.

In his absence, I was forced into decisions only to have him stop by just long enough to undermine them. "Well, I wouldn't have done what you did," he'd say when I protested; it didn't occur to him to support my action, telling me that he disagreed with me, even asking me not to do it again, but seeing me through it once it was done. So certain did he appear of his essential rectitude on these occasions that I could never disagree with him without being made to feel—after a while a single stony glance would do the trick—foolish, guilty, difficult, mean, hysterical. Years later, when he finally began to open himself to me, he explained that his absences, silences, and contradictions had arisen not so much from self-righteousness as from uncertainty and confusion, which society did not permit him even to feel, much less to acknowledge. As an adult male, he was required to take command, do the right thing, or else lose face. Since he didn't know what to do with the children any more than I did but couldn't afford to betray his ignorance, he fled. Later, he could approve or disapprove my decisions; and since the disapprovals rankled, those are the ones I remember. But of course! Illuminated by this fresh knowledge, huge chunks of our past—baffling and bitter—fall into interpretable patterns.

Too late for the children, though, who have struck out into the world bearing their birthright of bumbles and blunders. If only we could have them back as babies today, now that we have some idea what to do with them. . . . But no. They're so fine as they are that they don't need another go-round. Children must be designed to survive and transcend parental fault the way desert vegetation endures drought: Anne and Matthew aren't even spindly and scraggly. After two years in Zaïre teaching farmers how to raise fish for food, Anne returned to Tucson and married another Peace Corps Volunteer; she teaches composition while working toward a master's in teaching English as a second language, and Eric is earning a doctorate in biochemistry. Matthew and Poppy, who have been together since they were fifteen, were married last year; Poppy cares for a quadriplegic man, and Matthew, who plays rock and classical bass, has finished an associate's degree in music. Where there were once two children, now there are four, and I imagine that one day there'll be even more, who will no doubt also endure and thrive while Anne and Eric and Matthew and Poppy dither through the fens and thickets where George and I once lurched lost and footsore, emerging at last into this sunlit space, everyone—miraculously—accounted for and in one piece.

If parenthood taxed us so, you'd think George and I might have had the sense not to have any more children. And in truth we never intended to have more children. We were careful not to conceive again after Matthew's problematic birth and especially after my multiple sclerosis was diagnosed. Following a pregnancy scare, George volunteered to have a vasectomy. Although we weren't Catholics at the time, it wouldn't have mattered if we had been, since we believe that the Church's condemnation of birth control not only intrudes upon personal conscience but actually interferes with responsible behavior toward God's creation. Why would anyone want us to produce a damaged child or a child whose mother was too ill to care properly for her?

When young, I'd been told that Catholics under the direction of the pope conspired to take over the world through their continual breeding, but no one pointed out that the conspirators were rich white men in long dresses and beanies whereas the tools of conspiracy were women, most plentifully poor brown women staggering through their eighth, or twelfth, or twentieth pregnancies who prayed to the Blessed Mother of an only child (for so the Church insists) to send a little rice, a little beans, maybe a chicken for Sunday. The issue has never really been one of quantity but of control: not more Catholics but "good" Catholics, docile and too exhausted to resist the domination of those who claim (through the merits of a bit of flesh dangling between their legs which they're forbidden to touch) privileged access to God. A woman who controls something as essential as her own procreative processes might prove unbiddable in other matters as well. She might reach out to God directly; then what power would a mediator possess?

Through its prohibition on birth control, the Church has suggested that the only right way to have children is through biological reproduction: a kind of forced labor culminating in the production of another soul for God. What kind of a God stands like Lee Iacocca at the end of an assembly line, driving his workers with a greedy "More! More!" while the automobiles pile up in showrooms and on freeways and in used-car lots and finally junkyards, his only satisfaction the gross production figures at the end of every quarter? The human race may once have needed conserving and augmenting through conception, pregnancy, and childbirth, but that project has succeeded rather too well. I've had a little experience in these matters (vastly more than the pope, the cardinals, the archbishops and bishops, or your local parish priest, all of whom might benefit from a few good years of nonsymbolic fatherhood), and I can tell you that there are all kinds of ways to have children, no worse than the biological route and possibly better, since God requires not merely that we produce children but that we care properly for the ones already here. In a world of finite resources, this task may now necessitate voluntary limitations on reproduction.

I'm not proposing that we should call an abrupt halt to the birds and bees business. On the contrary, in spite of my bitching, I'm thrilled to have borne and raised Anne and Matthew. Personally, I've been forced into the kinds of growth I couldn't have experienced otherwise; and the world has gained two splendid presences. I wouldn't ask anyone to forgo such joy. But I do think that we should de-emphasize biology as the basis for forming authentic families. We should stop making those incapable of reproduction feel so guilty and deprived that they go to sometimes quite crazy lengths to get a baby in a socially acceptable form, a "real" baby. And we should encourage those who responsibly elect to produce only one or two offspring to ask themselves whether their family is quite big enough or whether it could benefit from just one more.

As for George and me, our habit has been to acquire new family members in their teens or early twenties, which saves on diapers and strained peas but offers its own sort of challenges. Child-rearing may be demanding, difficult, even on occasion downright crazy-making, but at least if you've been in the company of this creature from the moment of conception (or, in the case of many adoptions, a few days after birth), you have had continual opportunity to adjust to its idiosyncrasies; in fact, you may be partly responsible for those idiosyncrasies. If the creature shows up on your doorstep at the age of twenty-one, some other mother may have adjusted beautifully to its idiosyncrasies but you most certainly have not. And all the good will in the world will not stop you from moments of wishing that that other mother had strangled it at birth. But in time you learn to accept these murderous fantasies as natural and let them drift through your consciousness and on out into whatever ether safely holds all our murderous fantasies at a distance from our active lives.

Take our "youngest." When the little house in our backyard which I now use as a studio fell vacant in 1988, I wondered whether it might be useful to a shelter for battered women as a means of extending the stay of someone who needed more than the two or three weeks most shelters can offer before she struck out on her own. Liking the idea, George called the Tucson Shelter for Women and Children. The woman there was non-committal, of course (who wouldn't be when some guy calls up looking for a woman to live in his little house?), but we've lived in the community long enough to be easy to check on, as she did, and shortly she suggested a young woman with a year-old baby. A baby? This is a little house, mind you. A little, little house. Just a room with a three-quarter bath and a closet. Of course, she'd have access to kitchen and laundry facilities in the "big" house, which is itself what many would call little, but her private space would be extremely cramped. But sure, she could come take a look. You can say this about acquiring children by this method: it doesn't take nine months, and it's painless. That very evening our family grew by two: Sylvia and Shane.

Not that we exactly knew what had happened right away. We'd offered shelter for a few weeks, which is time enough to begin a friendship but not to extend a family. When Sylvia said she needed a place until she finished business school in June, we suggested that she try it for a month; if she and Shane weren't totally squirrelly at the end of that time, she could stay on, paying us rent of a hundred dollars a month out of her welfare check. In this way, we hoped that she'd feel entitled to the space, not admitted to it at the sufferance of Lord and Lady Bountiful. Issues of dependence and self-sufficiency invariably arise with adult children, even children you don't yet recognize as yours, and we wanted Sylvia to understand that we believed her capable of providing for herself and Shane. She didn't always pay her rent on time, and sometimes she had to borrow some of it back, but on balance she met this responsibility fully.

Another thing about getting children this way: it's gradual. You can't be a little bit pregnant, and once you are pregnant, the condition doesn't generally escape your notice; but you may become a foster parent, at least in the informal way George and I have done it, in increments too small to distract you from whatever else you think you're doing at the time. The few weeks we'd offered in September stretched into nine months. Then the business school that had promised to train Sylvia and find her a terrific job by June persuaded her that she couldn't possibly find a *really* terrific job without more training, so she borrowed several thousand dollars more for tuition and signed on till March. This was a scam (as became clear when the school didn't even try to find her a job of any sort), but she was too insecure to resist, and suddenly nine months promised to be eighteen.

In the end, Sylvia was one of our family (but by no means the only one) who needed a nudge out of the nest. Well, more like a hearty heave. Although we gave her six months' notice, allowing her plenty of time to plan had she been so inclined, her circumstances had made her hesitant, timid. Because her divorced mother had never been well, their roles had often been reversed; Sylvia fled this burdensome relationship straight into the arms of a man even more childish; at the time she fled his beatings, she and Petey and five-month-old Shane were living in his car. Through a special program at the shelter, she'd stayed seven months instead of one, but seven months is not an adequate childhood. As part of our family, she could go on, for a while, letting down her guard.

For me, Sylvia had come at a good time. Just a few months younger than Anne, who had gone off to Zaïre the year before, she was bright and affectionate. I was lonely for a daughter, someone to whom I could give pretty clothes and makeup and the quantities of gratuitous advice that had been building up like water on the brain. Although the little house was theirs, she and Shane spent most of their waking hours in the big one, and the presence of a toddler could be terrifically trying, but we were never burdened by his care. On the contrary, Sylvia relieved us of burdens, competently managing the household for us whenever we went away. And traveling is more fun when you've got children to take presents home to.

Sylvia finally graduated. After a couple of temporary and unsatisfactory living arrangements, she found an apartment for herself and Shane. Eventually she found a job, which she kept until the recession caused the firm to lay off two-thirds of its staff; then another, which she lost when she got pregnant again; now, she's back on public assistance, the father of this child no more inclined to provide for it than Petey was to support Shane. We feel as angry and disappointed as any parents would at her self-limiting behavior, but now seems the worst of times to reject her and Shane, and anyway, how could we get them out of our hearts? So we continue our intermittent phone calls and get-togethers. Each time Shane arrives, he seems another half a head taller, too big really for the little chairs that were once Anne and Matthew's, but he drags one out and scrunches into it, chin on knees, as he brings us up to date on cultural developments we've missed, like Inspector Gadget and the Teenage Mutant Ninja Turtles, one of whom (I'm not sure which, but it can't have been Hieronymous Bosch or I'd remember) absolutely had to appear on the pair of shoes George took him to buy last week or else he would go barefoot from here to eternity.

"How many children do you have?" people ask, and I have to say, "Well, it depends on what you mean by children. . . ." There are Ron and Angel and Alex and C.J. Anne and Eric. Matthew and Poppy. Sylvia and Shane and whoever the new baby will be. In time, these may produce even more, but George and I are in such fragile health now that I don't foresee our taking in any others from the outside. I'm not making any promises, though. Accidents happen.

Of late, a terrific hue and cry has been raised by political conservatives about "family values." Although these words are general to the point of inanity, few people ask for definitions specific enough to determine whether what a speaker means by "family" and "values" matches their own understanding. The followers of Charles Manson identified themselves as a family, after all; so strong is the religio-familial sense among the Mafia that they call their leaders "godfathers"; murder and mayhem may be just as highly prized as any other fun for the whole family. All the same, when some handsome blond politician of relatively few years and even fewer brains fulminates about the return to traditional "family values" in a sound bite on the nightly news, I know the family he has in mind: a daddy who works for wages outside the tidy white house with the two-car garage, a mummy who works for room and board inside it, two-point-something children, a fluffy cat and a spotted dog, and a cookie-baking grandma in a flowered apron who lives far enough away to render occasional visits a treat. Daddy hasn't lost his job in the copper mine, and Mummy has never attempted suicide. Dick hasn't just come out of the closet; Jane isn't scheduled to have an abortion in the morning; baby Sally wasn't born with cerebral palsy; the dog and cat have had their rabies shots; Grandma's intermittent lapses of memory don't signal the onset of Alzheimer's. And certainly a scrawny kid from a nearby detention center—no relation at all, not even a member of the same race—hasn't recently moved into the spare room and started classes at Dick and Jane's high school.

The millions of us who learned to read from the same primer all know the family, with its values of propriety and self-control, he envisions. But what can we make of his tone, so shrill and desperate that in a woman it might be called hysterical? What's he got at stake? "Expansive monarchs . . . valorized the patriarchal family," the historian Lois Banner writes, "as representing in miniature the centralized state, thereby positioning the father in the family as akin to the male monarch heading the state."[1] Once again, like Virginia Woolf in *Three Guineas* nearly sixty years ago, we uncover the complicity between the public and private spheres. In the absence of a throne, our Handsome Young Politician may aspire to an expansive presidency: the United States dominating the family of man, just as our HYP heads the United States, just as each man in the United States carries out his rightful (even God-given) role as paterfamilias. Thus, he extols traditional family values not because these are inherently good (goodness being a culturally based attribute) but because they replicate the power relationships on which his status depends. What's at *stake*? Only the world as we know it!

Another man, dark-skinned, dark-eyed, even younger than our HYP and something of a political klutz, once suggested that family might best not be based on blood ties at all. "My mother and my brothers," he said, "are those who hear the word of God and do it" (Luke 8.21): those who love God without restraint and their neighbors as themselves. The family, the microcosm into which we're born, inevitably serves as the model for our wider systems of relationships, and those of us who want a genuinely new world order—equitable, inclusive, tolerant, pacific, filled with jokes and festivals—must develop our ideas about family, and our families themselves, in the light of that correlation. There really is a human family (even in the genetic sense, our mitochondrial DNA having come to us through our mothers all the way from some primordial Eve), for which we need a new family order. What's at stake here is not the-world-as-we-know-it but the world. Period.

Toward this end, I must confess, the Mairs family, which is in most respects about as conventionally middle-American as you can get, has taken only a couple of tottering steps, and for this reason, I sometimes hesitate to say much about us even as I long, through sharing our experiences, to encourage others to unfold and enrich their lives by opening their families as we have done. This is a tricky point, this matter of public disclosure, one on which Jesus isn't entirely helpful: "Beware of practicing your piety before men in order to be seen by them," he cautions, yet within the same sermon he says, "Let your light so shine before men, that they may see your good works and give glory to your Father who is in heaven" (Matt. 5–7). If I write about my heterodox motherhood, an act that I certainly intend to be "seen" by men, and women too, am I parading my piety, or am I providing them a chance to glorify the holy? Probably, my experience of Christian moral practice tells me, both. Just to be on the safe side, since I've always found self-righteousness at least as seductive as sex, I take Jesus literally: "No one is good but God alone" (Mark 10.18). Whatever you see in me, it's not piety.

I'm not being cute here, brushing aside my maternal life with a blush and a flick of the wrist: "Oh, pshaw, it's really nothing." Childcare is never *nothing*. I just don't see anything praiseworthy in doing no more than one believes one is required to do. On this point Jesus is perfectly explicit: "Whoever receives one such child in my name receives me"; and whoever "receives me, receives not me but him who sent me" (Matt. 18.5, John 13.20). God has come here to me in the form of newborn infants and abandoned adolescents and unwed mothers, draped in chains and padlocks with a razor blade dangling from one ear, breaking my crockery, staining the floral chintz of my favorite couch, planting sticky kisses on my lips and eyeglasses, waving goodbye on the way to kindergarten, to boot camp, to Iceland or Africa. It is not a wonder that I have taken God in but a scandal that I have received God so infrequently and grumpily. Nevertheless, God's house is commodious, Jesus has assured me, and when the time comes for her to return my dubious hospitality, I have every reason to believe that she, of all beings, can always find room for one more.

PART THREE

Now

and

Forever

FROM MY HOUSE TO MARY'S HOUSE

"Charity" is a tricky concept. At its root, which it shares with "cherish," the word suggests no ordinary, indiscriminate affection but the love of something precious (costly, dear). Why then has it come to imply condescension? As with so many other ideas pertaining to relationships, our vast cultural passion for hierarchy must be at work. And where did that come from, I often wonder: out of the forest primeval, where if I perched in a tree while you skulked on the ground, I could more readily make you my lunch than you could make me yours? But that was quite a while ago.

161

My mouth no longer waters when I glimpse you, even at lunchtime. Isn't it time we dismantled a structure that so poorly organizes human interactions? Not that this would be an easy task. Our language, and the consciousness it shapes, is permeated with figures of domination and subordination so thoroughly that if we tried to extricate them, the whole fabric might unravel and leave us gibbering, unable to construct a single coherent thought.

It's a risk we'll have to take, I think, if we are to survive as recognizably human(e) beings in a world of finite resources. Of course, nothing guarantees that we *are* to survive, and a good bit of recent evidence suggests that we aren't, but I think we ought to give survival a shot. I'm not talking about "hanging in there." I'm not talking about a few minor adjustments, or even a lot of major adjustments. I'm not talking about a new world order that permits Iraqi women and children to be bombed at the command of rich white men just as Vietnamese women and children were under the old world order, only more efficiently and with wider approval. I am talking about an upheaval so radical that it exalts every valley and makes the rough places a plain, not along the San Andreas Fault but in the human psyche, which will no longer choose (not desire—it may well still desire—but choose) to organize itself and its relationships with others in terms of power and rank.

We might begin where all things begin, with God. We need to revise the language we use to conceptualize God in relation to ourselves. No more "Lord" and "Master." No more "thrones" or "principalities." No more oracular pronouncements "from on high." God with (in, among, beside, around, not over and above) us. This is one of the reasons that I've trained myself (and I balked badly at first) to refer to God with the feminine pronoun. I don't think God is a woman, any more than I think she's a man, but we're stuck with a gendered language: God has got to be he, she, or it. As a woman, I now feel most comfortable with "she" because traditionally in my culture women have not occupied positions of political dominance, associations with which might corrupt my experience of the holy, and because I identify with her, thus becoming aware of her presence in me, more readily when I use the same pronoun generally used for me. For a long time I considered changing "God," trying out "Goddess," "Holy One," "Yahweh," and the like, but they always felt contrived. Sometimes repeating "God" instead of using any pronoun is effective, but frequent repetitions at short intervals, by calling attention to themselves, distract me. The shift to the feminine pronoun seems to do the trick.

The purpose in finding a comfortable mode of address is to become aware of God drawn "down" into the midst of us, by whatever means will work. If she abides there, then the love we feel both for her and for one another as we embody her moves laterally, not hierarchically, and charity can never be tainted by condescension. When I use the word, I never intend it to suggest the act of a "do-gooder" who gives a "hand-out" or a "hand-me-down" to someone "less fortunate" than himself; no matter what decency and good will both donor and recipient may feel, that "less" in the consciousness of one or both ineluctably skews their relationship. Charity is not a matter of degree. It is never nice. It wells up out of a sense of abundance, spilling indiscriminately outward. True, your abundance may complement someone else's lack, which you are moved to fill, but since your lacks are being similarly filled, perhaps by the same person, perhaps by another, reciprocity rather than domination frames the interchanges. Some people may be "more" fortunate and some "less," by whatever standard you choose. But absolutely everybody has abundances.

Of course, an abundance may not take a form you much like. I recall stopping, one blazing afternoon several years ago, at the Time Market for a carton of milk. Outside I was approached by a man wearing few clothes and fewer teeth and a lot of sweat (life on the street in Tucson in midsummer is grueling), who asked me for a dollar. In those days, I didn't give money to people on the street because I knew they'd spend it on booze and I felt guilty assisting their addiction. Later, I was persuaded by the example of my beloved mentor Jerry Robinett that my task was to give what I was asked for, leaving responsibility for the use of my gift to its recipient. But on this day I still thought of myself as a moral guardian, so I shook my head. Inside, as was my habit when I'd been panhandled, I bought in addition to my milk a large apple and a granola bar (oh, the smugness of us virtuous types—why the hell not a red Popsicle and a Twinkie?).

When I offered these to the man outside, he snarled and turned his back. He'd been joined by a friend, who said to him quietly, "You know her. From the Casa. Go on and take them." He just shook his head, so I extended them to the friend, who took them and smiled. There was genuine grace in his gesture, his reluctance to hurt the feelings of a woman he'd seen at the soup kitchen, and I welcomed that gift from his abundance. But the other had an abundance, too—an abundance of resentment—from which he'd given just as freely. I was chastened by the gift, by his refusal to say "Thank you, kind lady," accepting my stupid health food when all he really wanted was a cold six-pack. If he'd done that, I'd never have found out that I'd offered him the wrong thing. I might have gone on believing that poor people were obliged to take what I gave them, consider themselves lucky to get it, and probably thank me politely in the bargain. I never said you had to *like* getting your lacks filled. I just said that someone, out of his abundance, would take care of the job.

Under ordinary circumstances, our abundances need letting off, like steam, and the family model chosen by contemporary middle-class society, wherein the whole huge human family is fragmented into clusters of only a few members each, which are packed separately and antiseptically, like cans of peas or jars of pickles, into houses and apartments and minivans, lacks adequate amplitude and ventilation. Accumulated, hoarded, our abundances build up an excruciating pressure that we seek to relieve in material acquisition, but the relief this measure brings is always only temporary, and eventually we find ourselves stopped up and sick with things.

I'm not preaching from a lofty perch here, looking down in pity on the rest of you poor fools gagging on your glut. I'm gasping claustrophobically under the weight of my own heap of possessions. Look! Down here! Under the three pairs of boots and the second television set! Admittedly, the boots are different colors to complement different articles in my wardrobe, and the television is a black-and-white portable with a five-inch screen: I'm a practical accumulator. But maybe color-coordination is not a laudable end or even a reasonable goal; and no one except my sports-crazy stepfather attempts to watch more than one television at a time. What am I really doing with all this stuff?

I know what I should do with it. I accept Jesus's admonition to the rich young man: "If you would be perfect, go, sell what you possess and give to the poor, and you will have treasure in heaven; and come, follow me" (Matt. 19.21). I know that such actions can be carried out, because I have friends who have done so. And I like to think I have developed to the point that, if only I were healthy and vigorous, I could do the same. If only. . . . Here's where I get stuck. I am too debilitated now to hold a job or even to care fully for myself. My husband has metastatic melanoma. When he dies, the modest resources we've accumulated may not even provide for my shelter and custodial care. If I were to give them away, then I'd become a public burden, worse than useless even to the poor I sought to serve. Conserving them seems less like greed than like social responsibility. And so I get off lightly. I can indulge in the fantasy that, under different circumstances, I would be "perfect" without ever having to put myself to the test: a saint manquée.

Well, what I would do if I could we'll never know. I must do what I can. Carrying out the injunction that closes every Mass, to "go in peace to love and serve God and our neighbor," takes the form of the works of mercy, seven of which are "corporal": (1) to feed the hungry, (2) to give drink to the thirsty, (3) to clothe the naked, (4) to visit the imprisoned, (5) to shelter the homeless, (6) to visit the sick, and (7) to bury the dead. Another seven are "spiritual": (1) to admonish the sinner, (2) to instruct the ignorant, (3) to counsel the doubtful, (4) to comfort the sorrowful, (5) to bear wrongs patiently, (6) to forgive all injuries, and (7) to pray for the living and the dead. "As far as I can tell, I'm supposed to do all of these," I say to George, "but some of the spiritual ones make me uneasy. They seem so presumptuous." He nods as I go on: "I'd rather just clothe the sinner"—we burst out laughing and say together—"and admonish the naked."

Seriously, at the risk of spiritual dereliction, I think I'll leave admonishment to someone with more of a flair for it and stick with bodies, their shelter and nurture and dispatch, for which a quarter of a century of mothering all creatures great and small has better fitted me. Let me feed the hungry. Let me clothe the naked (and sinners too). I won't do it well or often enough, I know from experience, but charity isn't a competition to be judged by the Big Examiner in the Sky, who'll knock off seven years of purgatory for every sack of groceries you drop off at the Community Food Bank. Nobody's looking. It's more like a game in which everyone gets a turn, or a dance for which everyone can choreograph a few steps. Even a woman too crippled to tie her own boots or drive a car can, at least if she has a partner who shares her sense of plenty, find a place in the vast web of transactions that binds and sustains the human family.

In such exchanges, no matter how equitable, the power of the giver to dispense or withhold some good is subtly privileged over the right of the receiver to accept or reject the offering by the fact of possession: you've got what I need. Even though I've long understood this distinction, only in recent years have I felt its force. What I need—repetitively, interminably—is help in performing even the most elementary tasks. I can't butter my own bread. Before long I may not even be able to use the toilet by myself. My dependency, in resembling that of a very young child, makes me feel demeaned, diminished, humiliated. This is a horrible situation, one that wracks me with grief and fury for which no socially acceptable outlet exists. What am I going to do if you offer to button my coat, after all—bite your fingers and then freeze to death? Of course not. I'm going to permit you to clothe the naked.

Horrible situations have their uses, however. Mine, in depriving me of the status associated with personal control, has forced humility upon me. I cannot patronize the poor. I am one of the poor. Currently my poverty isn't economic, though it may one day be that as well, but its effects are similar. I must be not only the agent but the object of the works of mercy. I must discipline myself to accept and welcome others' care. I wish I could tell you that I'm doing a terrific job of it, that I'm just the sweetest, humblest little woman you've ever met, but I can't. All

I can say is that, in learning to give care whenever I can and receive care whenever I must, I've grown more attentive to the personal dimension of the works of mercy.

So accustomed are most of us to thinking of human neediness not in personal but in economic terms that, asked for a charitable donation, we reflexively whip out our checkbooks and pens. Writing a check to a "charity" is not on the list of the works of mercy, however. It's a generous act, one that ought to be performed as frequently as the budget will bear, but it can't substitute spiritually for direct engagement with people in need. "Poverty" and "affliction" and "oppression" are abstractions whose remedy might seem to lie in the intangible transfer of a monetary amount from one account to another. Poor and afflicted and oppressed people have faces, and we are required to look squarely into them. We can't love what we won't experience. For this reason, George and I have always sought to make our charity concrete.

Although our most sustained and intimate charitable relationships have grown out of taking people into our home, not everyone has the physical plant or the emotional resources to make room for one more, and currently that includes us. Over the years, however, we've discovered other ways of developing caring relationships, making us, I suppose, one of those "thousand points of light" upon which conservative politicians have wished like stars in recent years. What speechwriter, I wonder, came up with an estimate so small in a country so vast, evoking brave scattered flickers of individual endeavor in the very heart of darkness?

Beneath such a metaphor lies a shift from public to private torch-bearing which suggests that the government can just excuse itself from tending to messy human needs and get on with protecting oil supplies and national security and the "American" flag (as though ours were the only one) and capital gains and other things that matter. In this model, even when human beings enter the government's purview, they tend to do so as things, not people. The unborn child—as yet untouched, invisible—must have the government's protection, but the embraceable infant, demanding breast milk and then a warm snowsuit and later textbooks and finally a steady job, gets thrust into the arms of one of us blinking lights. Unless by acting up she converts herself back into a thing—goes on a murderous shooting spree and has to be put to death, say, or fails to pay her taxes—the government will scarcely concern itself with her again.

This model has served us badly, and will continue to serve us badly, because it draws a false distinction between private and public concerns and between personal and governmental responsibility for coping with them. No things matter, either publicly or privately, except as they preserve and enhance the intricate process that I would call God's creation. All actions, both public and private, have equal impact, for good or ill, on that process. And no one, not even a dim bulb like George Bush, is excused from equal participation in it. We all lead lives of public service, and at last count, there should have been about 250 million points of light in the United States alone, plenty for a conflagration.

Individually and collectively, we must take on the tasks at hand, imbuing them with the reciprocity that arises out of our various abilities and diverse requirements. Until a few years ago, for instance, I refused to hire help around the house because I couldn't stand the thought of making someone my "servant"; eventually, with George teaching in two programs and my physical condition deteriorating, I was forced to find a weekly housekeeper or suffocate under a drift of grease, desert dust, and corgi hair. At this point, the mistress/servant model no longer represented my reality. Because the need my house-keeper has for the money I pay her is no greater than my need for assistance, our dependence is mutual.

And our relative authority must be balanced accordingly. Since I can not clean my own house, it has become to some extent no longer my *own* house. It has slipped from my control, a very good thing, since Celia takes far better care of it than I would have done even in the days when my arms and legs still worked. She cleans between all the buttons on the antiquated push-button stove so that our fingers no longer stick and release with a schloop every time we want to go from hot to warm. She keeps the sliding-glass door so clean that, after my daughter walked through and shattered it, we had to paste a hedgehog decal onto the new one to ward off future incursions. But she does not know where things "belong," like the fish-shaped soup tureen on the sideboard; although this "should" be placed side-ways, she invariably points its pouty face out into the room. At first I'd turn it back after she left; later, when I got too weak, I'd simply look at it and fret; at length, insight struck: *Whoa, wait a minute! Whose fish is this anyway?* It's mine, I know. When my friend Mollie left Tucson, she gave it to me to hold until her return, but she liked Seattle better and I've got the fish by de-fault. But it's Celia's fish, too, she's the one who takes care of it, and apparently it "should" stare out at us broodily even though I think it looks dopey that way.

To relinquish not merely control but the claim to control, permitting someone to do what she does best in the way she chooses to do it and viewing the outcome as collaborative rather than "right" or "wrong," balances a relationship that might otherwise be skewed by issues of ownership or preroga-tive. Celia and I have a hollow cream-colored stoneware fish. If you want to help us with its upkeep, you may have it, too. If no one drops it, it will outlast both Celia and me. One day, however, it's bound to be smashed, and then no one will have it anymore. Things come to us, and we cherish them for a while, and then they or we are gone. When Jesus says, "You cannot serve both God and mammon," it is not the thinginess of our possessions he repudiates but our relationship to them: the way that, instead of simply tending them and putting them to use, we grasp them with knuckles turned white, clasp them against our chests, invest them with the power to represent our worth. Perhaps for this reason the early Christians held their goods in common: so that they wouldn't be tempted into controlling one another through commodities.

As valuable as personal relationships like mine with Celia are in transforming abstract works of mercy into concrete expressions of love, in the end you cannot know every person you serve. Lacks are too great; energies are too limited; and anyway, just as some donors prefer to remain anonymous, so do some recipients. To serve such needs on a large scale requires a whole charitable community like Casa María, which runs Our Lady of Guadalupe Chapel and Free Kitchen. At the core of this community, which occupies several small houses on Tucson's south side, are Brian Flagg, voluble and hyperkinetic, and George Pettit, soft-spoken but equally fierce in his commitment, his wife, Debbie, and their baby, Catie, together with several veterans of life on the streets: Lonnie, Lowell, Andy, Bill. These now form our family, too. With them we celebrate marriages and baptisms and birthdays, attend rallies and marches and vigils, and get arrested for civil disobedience, to the consternation of some of our less radical relatives.

Although, in order to avoid the NIMBY syndrome that has closed down similar projects around town, Casa María is a consecrated chapel, where Mass is said every Monday morning, no one is required to pray for her or his supper. Holding fast to the thousand-points-of-light principle, the federal government no longer contributes surplus goods like cheese, and operating expenses have soared to about seven thousand dollars a month. The program subsists on donations of money, food, and time from all over Tucson and even beyond: The last time I was there I met several Mennonite grandmothers from the Midwest who spend three months in Tucson every winter; while they make and bag sandwiches, their husbands do home repairs for poor people. Established just over ten years ago for the explicit purpose of performing works of mercy, Casa María initially served one meal a day—soup, a couple of sandwiches, fruit, a sweet, coffee, and milk when available for the children—to a couple of hundred people. On a recent Saturday the number was thirteen hundred. Although the number of single men has stayed stable for several years, more and more families have come as the realities of Reagan-Bush economics have taken hold even here in the supposedly recession-proof Southwest.

"All those people want is a free ride," a woman at an adult-education conference told me over dinner a couple of years ago when I mentioned my involvement with Casa María. "I have to drive by that soup kitchen on my way to work, and I've seen them lined up three times a day waiting for their handouts."

"Odd," I said. "The soup kitchen serves only lunch."

"Well, whatever. I see them there, just hanging around. They don't even want to find work."

"That's true," I said. "Some of them don't. And some are too sick to work. But some of them do. They're all different. Why don't you stop on your way to work one day and ask them?" The question was rhetorical. I couldn't imagine why this woman drove by the soup kitchen, which is not on a main thoroughfare, but I could imagine how: locked tight in her car, as fast as she could get away with in a neighborhood heavily patrolled by the police and La Migra (Immigration and Naturalization Service). And who could blame her? Families there come and leave quickly. Most of the people hanging around the kitchen are men who, now that the old SRO (single room occupancy) hotels have been torn down to make room for luxury condominiums and motorways, live on the street. Unwashed, unshaven, in wardrobes chosen from the boxes of donated clothing Lonnie supervises, they look bad. (They can also smell bad, which is not a problem for this woman with her windows rolled up tight but is for me, afflicted with a hypersensitive nose, when I'm among them.) They tend to be grumpy, as you probably would be too if you sought your night's rest under the Murphy Overpass. A woman alone might well choose not to mingle in such company.

Her loss. I must sound supercilious, but I'm not. I mean she really has cheated herself of experience in the way we all do when we whiz past the world with the air conditioner pumping full-blast and the *Goldberg Variations* trilling from the tape deck. She has lost the opportunity to know a little more about the world: "know," that is, not in the way she "knows" that the people queued up outside the soup kitchen are freeloaders but in the way she "knows" Paris, say, having spent a summer there between her junior and senior years in college. We know the world, as God knows the world, only by entering it. Photos in *Newsweek* or *National Geographic* won't do. Editorials in *The Nation* or *The New Republic* won't do. Sixty-second clips on the nightly news about unemployment, homelessness, substance abuse, mental illness, and serial murderers won't do. You gotta *be* there.

And if you're there with even half an eye open, you see that nothing so simple as freeloading is going on. To begin with, nothing's being given out that would seduce you away from a regular paycheck. Except maybe the soup, which is generally excellent, hot and highly spiced. The sandwiches are most likely orange cheese-like food or peanut butter mixed with fruit cocktail on day-old bread. The apples and bananas are bruised. There might be a stale Ding-Dong or a Snickers bar, but if your teeth have rotted to stumps, these furnish more pain than pleasure. You can squat on the ground and eat this stuff if you can fend off the damned pigeons long enough. If you need to take a crap, there are a couple of portable toilets in one corner of the yard. If the soles of your boots have holes, Lonnie might be able to find a pair not quite as worn and more or less your size.

The lap of luxury doesn't draw these people, then. Some are temporarily down and out, but many are chronically hungry and/or homeless. The family bags usually go to people in the neighborhood who can afford either rent or food but not both. Of the people on the street, most are men, a disproportionate number of them Vietnam vets. A lot have fevers, wracking coughs, ulcerated legs and feet, abscessed teeth. Some drink, smoke marijuana, do heroin or cocaine. A few are crazy as bedbugs, "freed" from state institutions in the early seventies to be turned over to a community-based mental-health system that nobody ever got around to establishing. No amount of exhortation will make these people "better," to use the standard of my dinner companion, or "different," to use a less loaded word. Am I to say to the man who asks for a cigarette and, when I give it to him (a dubious charity, I'll admit), showers me with kisses and calls down the blessing of Cristo upon me: "Good God, man, pull up your socks and get right down to the Department of Economic Security for a job interview!?" Who the hell would want him around? I've had him around for at least five minutes now and *I* don't want him, I assure you.

At Casa María one learns, sooner or later depending upon one's resistances, that in spite of all our charitable efforts, some of the poor we will always have with us, just as Jesus warned, and our care for them can never cease. I'm no defeatist. In the decade George taught adult education, we saw person after person on public assistance earn a GED, attend community college, find a job, and become (a point of pride) a taxpayer; and if the government would hand us illuminati out here more funds, instead of blowing them on bomb tests and the bad debts of persons in high places, such successes could mount exponentially. But there will always be a Frances, wearing my white wool tam-o-shanter at a jaunty angle and leading on leashes her two pet chickens, invisible to the naked eye, around the encampment of homeless people at the county courthouse on Christmas Eve. Frances can't depend on herself; she can't even depend on the damned chickens, who disappear unpredictably even from her view. At the least, she ought to be able to depend on me.

Wholehearted commitment to people who are poor, afflicted, or oppressed, although it inevitably necessitates political choices and leads to shared political action, must first be rooted in personal conversion, described by the liberation theologist Leonardo Boff as follows: "The conversion demanded by Jesus is more than a mere change of conviction—a change in theory. It is also, and mainly, a change of attitude—a change bearing directly on practice. Nor is it a change only within a person—a change of heart. It is also a change in that person's living, functioning network of relationships."[1] Not by chance, I think, was Dorothy Day, the founder of the Catholic Worker movement, a convert to Roman Catholicism. Every Frances necessitates a new and conscious conversion—a turning again to enter communion at each fresh encounter—for which Dorothy showed an extraordinary gift. One needn't be a Catholic, or even a Christian, in order to undergo such change or carry out such action, of course; but one must by some means learn the habit of turning toward and taking in.

The charity that begins at home cannot rest there but draws one inexorably over the threshold and off the porch and down the street and so out and out and out and out into the world which becomes the home wherein charity begins until it becomes possible, in theory at least, to love the whole of creation with the same patience, affection, and amusement one first practiced, in between the pouts and tantrums, with parents, siblings, spouse, and children. Relationship: connection: kinship: family: love: the movement from an abstract and emotionless awareness that there are needy people out there to the give-and-take—tender, quarrelsome, jokey, impassioned—of siblings crowded together under the roof of Mary's House. The choice to name Casa María for La Virgen de Guadalupe is especially apt, not only because she is the patron saint of Mexico, only seventy miles from Tucson, but because she appeared to a poor man of questionable mental stability: the Queen of Heaven placed a rose in the hands of a bemused peasant. In charity distances dissolve. As a response to the gratuitous outpouring of God's love, charity demands that one turn one's face toward the face of an other and confront there both oneself and God.

GOD'S WILL

🔥

A couple of years ago, I had an experience that struck me, in spite of its familiar setting and maybe even, in some people's lives, its predictability, as odd. I was at the Newman Center Mass I often attend on Saturday afternoons. Still walking in those days, I had just received communion and returned to my pew, where I knelt and, after one coherent little prayer, began the interior jumble that forms my post-communion meditation. This was even more of a mess than usual because I felt panic-stricken: my multiple sclerosis was getting worse, almost by the day, and my resolve to cope bravely, in a manner befitting my stern Yankee heritage, was weakening even faster than my muscles were. I just wanted to get rid of the damned disease. "God, God, God," I prayed, "please, heal me!" And then, for the first and only time in my life, I got a response. I'd never heard voices, and I didn't hear one now. Three monosyllables simply materialized in my consciousness: "But I am."

I'm no mystic, although when I was much younger, especially while I was reading Dame Julian of Norwich and St. John of the Cross, I wished that I were one. In later years I've come to think it's just as well that I'm not. If I had a mystical experience—saw Jesus, say, or felt his hand in mine—I'd behave badly, I suspect: screech, the way I do when a spider surprises me, or faint away. And yet, that once, those words formed; and I accepted them. I took them into my life. I didn't understand, and still don't, what they mean: how an relentless degeneration of my central nervous system can function to "heal" me. But I had no trouble recognizing the message, or believing it. Why not? I wondered then. I still do.

I'd asked for the wrong thing, of course. What I wanted, plainly and simply, was to be cured of MS: to arise from my pew on two strong legs and stride firmly out into the world, where I would once again go dancing, ride a bicycle, maybe even learn to ski, resume needlework and calligraphy, and then join the Peace Corps for the grand adventure of my life. Since "cure" and "heal" can be used interchangeably, I didn't reflect before making my choice. Their meanings are subtly different, however. What I had asked for was not to be freed from my limp or my nasty habits, which might be effected instantaneously, but to be made whole, which might entail collecting scattered fragments and painstakingly fitting and gluing them into place. The one occurrence is not necessarily more miraculous than the other, but the drama of it—the paralytic rising to his feet and trudging with his pallet past the outraged scribes, Lazarus staggering from the cave's mouth in his stinking grave-clothes—distracts and delights as healing's tedium cannot do.

I believe in those spectacular curative miracles. I also believe that Emma Woodhouse married Mr. Knightley at last and Emma Bovary gulped handfuls of arsenic and died in writhing agony, events that have no claim on historicity at all, and so my belief may reveal more about the habits of a student of literature than about religious faith. We students are not, when you come right down to it, models of rationality. Otherwise, I would probably try to explain the miracles away—the blind man was merely hysterical, his eyesight restored by the power of suggestion; spooked by an unseen wolf, the swine pell-melled like lemmings into the sea—anything to avoid looking a gullible fool. But fretting over whether these miracles "really" occurred misses the point: a very long time ago, a person came into the world whose actions and utterances so amazed the people around him by their divine implications that they never forgot them. In view of the frailty of human memory, something extraordinary happened and has gone on happening to this day: Emmanu-el: God With Us. What better grammar than miracles for communicating such an astounding state of affairs?

And so I willingly believe in signifying miracles of this sort. But I also believe that they are very, very rare. I do not expect one to happen to me. Some would say that through skepticism I disqualify myself, that if only I had faith as a grain of mustard seed I could be cured, but I don't have faith as a grain of mustard seed, I don't have faith as a paramecium or even a quark, so I'll just have to go on as I am. (There are, I'm willing to bet, worse ways to be, though you wouldn't know from the amount of complaining I do that I thought so.) God is no White Knight who charges into the world to pluck us like distressed damsels from the jaws of dragons, or diseases. God chooses to become present to and through us. It is up to us to rescue one another.

"I love how ordinary some of the miracles are," George tells me. "Feeding multitudes with a few loaves and a couple of fishes. Any of us could do it." He knows whereof he speaks. Our friend Kansas has just called to report he's retrieved a bounty of bags of potato chips from the dumpster behind Fry's Supermarket, and can George drive them down to Casa María for Friday's lunches? Those potato chips were there not by the will of God, I'm sure, but by the will of the store manager who noticed the expiration date; and the hand of Kansas, not the hand of God, gleaned them. There is nothing supernatural at work here. *That's* the miracle: not that some unseen almighty force showers potato chips down upon our heads but that a man goes dumpster-diving and rescues the potato chips while most of them are probably still edible. Since this man does not want the potato chips for himself—he couldn't possibly consume them all—from a personal perspective his act is wholly gratuitous. It signifies love. Through performing this miracle over and over and over again, we are made whole.

"Ubi caritas et amor," the voices of the Community of Christ of the Desert chant as we pass the little basket of broken bread, the stoneware cup filled with red wine, each pausing to murmur *The Body of Christ, The Blood of Christ, Amen,* pausing to chew, pausing to sip, taking up the plain melody again, "ubi caritas, Deus ibi est." Where charity and love are, God is there.

In the midst of this community on the Easter before last, I had the only other experience that could even remotely be considered mystical. It occurred during the Vigil Mass, at which, as the Christ candle is brought into the church, we welcome light back into a world darkened by suffering and death and later, for the first time since the beginning of Lent, recite the Gloria. All of a sudden I knew that—here, now—I had entered the Kingdom of God. Or, more precisely, that the Kingdom of God had slipped in and settled around me. That, in fact, it had always done so without my ever quite catching sight of it before. The sensation wasn't markedly different from other experiences of intense relaxation and delight, and I knew that it wouldn't last. But I also knew that it would come back, that I could call it back, through my own attitudes and practices, and that through these I was helping to create the Kingdom for which Christians assiduously pray.

Most Christians will doubtless be startled not by my discovery but by the obtuseness with which I'd persisted, in the teeth of plenty of contrary evidence, in believing that the Kingdom was some utopian state to be brought about by the will of God at some indefinite moment in the future when God decided that we'd all become good enough to merit it. What, I wonder now, did I think "at hand" meant? Stretching out my hands, I can reach the Bible in my lap and, on my desk, my computer, my printer and the tottering pile of books on it, a forty-four-ounce Thirstbuster now sucked dry, a box of floppy disks, an old letter from Aunt Jane, and the trifocals I wear when I'm not peering at my monitor screen. This is at-handness: not what is about to be given us, but what is near enough to be grasped and used. The trick is not to squint hopefully into some distant future but to look around you: "The kingdom of God is not coming with signs to be observed; nor will they say, 'Lo, here it is!' or 'There!' for behold, the kingdom of God is in the midst of you" (Luke 17.20–21).

Until I recognized that I was, however fitfully, right in it, I didn't give much thought to the word "kingdom." Since I've never lived in a monarchy, the word held purely figurative meaning, and the figure had the virtue of familiarity. But custom doesn't provide the soundest basis for continuing to use any word, and "kingdom," with its overtones of both political and sexual inequities, is particularly problematic. Although some gender-conscious writers now use "reign," a simple shift to a Latinate root with the same meaning doesn't remove the taint of human power used by one individual to control others, a force utterly different from "the will of God." In order to recognize and celebrate God among us, we need a word that bespeaks another order. The Nation of God? Too jingoistic. The State of God? Too ambiguous, perhaps: one can, after all, be in the state of Arizona, a gaseous state, a distraught state, a deplorable state, as well as a state of grace. The City of God? Despite the dazzling imagery of Revelation, this seems too localized and distractingly mundane, calling to mind property taxes and weekly trash collections. For etymological reasons, I like the Commonwealth of God—the shared well-being it holds—but its general usage is too narrowly political. And so I settle, unoriginally but happily, for all the resonances of the Community of God.

"Thy community come. Thy will be done. . . . " These parallel subjunctive clauses can certainly be read as petitions for some vaguely political future arrangement in which, having miraculously all repented and amended our wicked ways, we find ourselves in a condition of conformity to God's will so perfect that we are vaulted into bliss forever. And here on earth, no less. Fat chance. There are several billion of us now, plundering one another's resources, starving one another's children and stealing one another's spouses, putting bombs in one another's autos and luggage and rice paddies, shooting one another with dirty syringes, Saturday night specials, SCUD missiles. We'll never all spontaneously stop sinning at the same time, even for an instant. Why even bother to pray for such an absurdity?

But suppose we are not meant to wait like docile children for God to make of us immaculate creatures worthy of some already created heaven that seems to hover relentlessly beyond our reach. Suppose that, never yet what we will be, we are meant to assist God in the creation of ourselves, in our own perfection, the process of making ourselves complete. Suppose God's Community comes not whenever God wills that it come but whenever God's will is done, and we're responsible for the doing. Suppose it can't happen without us: "God has not left us a finished world," Leonardo Boff writes, "but has willed to associate us to the task of transforming it."[1] Then prayer becomes more than hopeful. Prayer is generative. Through it we draw "earth" and "heaven" together into a new whole.

Ooh, this sounds nifty, positively New Age, all breathless enthusiasm and prettiness of vision. There's a hitch, though, and not a slight one. God's will. In the absence of God, who is in a totalized sense irretrievably absent from our limited consciousnesses, we can each claim to have discerned the will of God in whatever events and acts we are called upon to explain or justify. Since these commonly involve wholesale slaughter as the result of either natural phenomena—spews of volcanic lava, the chomping jaws of insects, stinking pestilences, scrawny plants withering in cracked earth—or human projects to exterminate people on the ostensible grounds that they are failing to perform God's will (though the true reason is generally that they are occupying territory the exterminators aim to possess), the portrait of God that emerges may overpower the squeamish.

"I just hate it when people say to me, 'God never sends us more than we can handle,'" complains one of the members of our Living with Cancer support group, whose husband died last year. "What kind of a God would *send* us sickness and pain?" What kind, indeed? And who could stay spiritually sane in relationship with a being of whose missives and projectiles one lived in dread? This matter is of more than idle interest to me, since I am forced to grapple with it moment by moment. Although I can't readily define what God wills, tainted as my vision is by the will of Nancy, I feel clearer about what God will(s) not, and hurling nastiness at us—as a test of faith, as a proof of power, or as a cosmic joke—heads the list. God has a sense of humor, to be sure (take a look at the blue-footed booby if you have doubts), but not at the expense of cripples.

Sometimes, when I am very angry, I imagine the Distant Trickster aloft, rocking and howling with laughter as I struggle to clothe my nakedness. "Are you having a good time?" I shout through the turtleneck in which my head is caught. "Are you amused up there, you and your blessed son? Ha ha." I drop the sock I'm trying with one hand to hook over my big toe. "Great fun, huh, watching a stupid cripple huff and sweat." My tone darkens. "I'm your creature, God. You're supposed to love me. WHY ARE YOU DOING THIS TO ME?" (With one of life's more excruciating perversities, the lid just popped off my daily Thirstbuster, dumping about a quart of Diet Coke onto the floor, and since I can't reach down to mop it up, I'll have to continue working on this passage with my feet in a sticky brown puddle.)

Sometimes my words degenerate into an infantile wail: "Whaaaaaaaaah!" But however I rail, no one is there. Or No One. Whatever. Multiple sclerosis is doing this to me, chewing up my central nervous system in a random reasonless process no God I could believe in could bring herself to inflict on me. To see myself as cosmically picked on requires me to reduce Godness to a human paradigm: the Bully and the Wimp, maybe, my snotty face scrubbed in the schoolyard dirt while I blubber for mercy. Of course, to think about God at all requires me to reduce her to one human paradigm or another, but at least I must choose one that rings intuitively true, and this one doesn't. Whatever the causes of my multiple sclerosis—a slow-acting virus triggering an aberrant autoimmune response to which a genetic mutation in a Northern European ancestor left me prone—they do not signify God in the world.

The cross signifies God in the world: God willing to take on human form and experience the full range of humanness, even death, in order to make clear to us our participation in divinity. Today is Ash Wednesday. For the next few weeks, I'll have ample time to reflect upon the cross, that locus of ignominy and suffering, the last place on earth anyone would look for God. But when you think about it, how else would God get into the world except through a radical revisionary with little regard for personal safety and a strong preference for the company of sinners, cripples, paupers, and women—"the poor and marginalized"[2]—to whom he promised redemption not so much from their own sins, toward which he was easier than many of his contemporaries approved, as from the injustices inflicted upon them by people with social, political, and religious power?

Imagine that God had tried to come as one of these last instead—Caiaphas, say, whose religious prominence might certainly have made him a likelier receptacle for divinity—the man would have been so smug, so full of himself to the very lip, that poor God couldn't have squeezed in with a shoehorn. And who'd have listened to him? "I love you"—Caiaphas would open his mouth and the words would pop out—"and I want you to love each other in the same way." How do you think the other priests of the Sanhedrin would take that? People with power do not just go around handing out stuff like love to any and all comers. They commodify and husband it, distributing it after due deliberation to the deserving (who are sometimes, but by no means frequently, poor). Nor are they likely to honor one of their number for writhing in death throes on a cross like a common criminal in front of God and everybody. And they expect any deity of theirs to exhibit the same thrift and propriety. They refuse to let God be who God will be.

God enters the world through those of us who are willing

to let God participate fully in our lives, in our sufferings as well as our celebrations. Through suffering with us, God empowers us to carry out the will of God: that we assume full responsibility not only for our own suffering but for the suffering of others. We are not pitiful creatures huddled helplessly beneath a blizzard of miseries blown down by some capricious power amusing himself at our expense. God is with(in) each of us, and to the extent that we recognize and honor God's presence in one another, we form and dwell in the Community of God.

Myself, I don't acknowledge this presence often, not nearly often enough to be doing my share in sustaining the Community of God. But the fact that I do it at all, however intermittently and imperfectly, tells me that it can be done. And the condition of the world tells me that it must be done, by as many of us as possible as continuously as possible, RIGHT NOW. We cannot afford to hang around praying for everybody else to see "the light," whatever that might be, and spontaneously beat their SCUDS into combines or their Patriots into reapers. *They are not going to do so,* all of them in an instant, not now, maybe never. Nor, if they haven't begun after nearly three millennia, are they about to impulsively "cease to do evil, learn to do good; seek justice, end oppression; defend the fatherless, plead for the widow" (Isa. 1.16–17). We can only clasp hands, take a deep breath, and plunge ahead with the faith "that the definitive goal—God, the reign of God, the Meaning of meanings—is already here in this very history, that God has begun to become reality in society itself, and that this occurs wherever just causes are fought for and realized."[3]

To hurtle headlong without regard for the odds of "success" seems especially urgent in the wake of the collapse of Communism. With the bifurcated vision and bloodthirstiness characteristic of patriarchally shaped consciousness, we've become so accustomed to the opposition Communism/capitalism that we perceive the demise of the one as a triumph for the other, without reflecting that because Communism and capitalism (and indeed most isms) are humanly reductive, viewing people as (re)productive and/or consumptive markers in a materially based economy, they are indistinguishably inadequate systems for containing and expressing the whole of experience. Indeed, we've declared victory to "the most complete and sophisticated and enduring form of totalitarianism which human social consciousness has yet devised. The only freedom guaranteed by capitalism is the freedom to acquire property."[4]

Not much of a bargain, it may turn out, sort of like trading a rotten halibut for a rotten haddock, but one that a good many powerful institutions, the Church among them, seem delighted to consummate, so thoroughly has Communism—poor sad system collapsing around its stinking entrails—been demonized. Some within those institutions may operate in full cynical awareness of the "causal relationship between the capitalistic mode of production and the generation of increasing misery,"[5] but the rest of us, with only the fuzziest understanding of economics, tend toward a genuine and even fervent conviction that the good guys have won and if all's not right with the world just yet, it soon will be.

As a woman who cannot balance her checkbook reliably, I'd be as ready to put my faith in the majestic and mysterious Market as the next guy if only the damned thing didn't have the whiff of jism about it: you know, the mentality that there's only so much to go around and if you come now you might not be able to get it up later so you'd better hang on to what you've got instead of giving it away. I'm fed up to the teeth with living in an economy based on male performance anxiety. I'll take as my model *jouissance*, its leisureliness, its amplitude, its generosity.

This is not a dog-eat-dog world (or even, as one of my students once wrote, a doggy dog world), in which terror over the scarcity of resources must lead to snarling and snatching. I have enough: time, love, experience, good advice, cats, and occasionally money. Don't you? If you don't, then I'll give to you from my surplus. If you do, then you must turn and give to someone else. Contrary to capitalistic myth, rapacity and greed are not elements in human nature (nor, perhaps, are any other qualities, so flexible is the human psyche) but maladaptive responses to the radical uncertainty of life. We can, through mutual encouragement, unlearn them, conforming instead to what Matthew Fox terms "the 'Eucharistic Law of the Universe'—a law that teaches that transformation and sacrifice, eating and being eaten, applies to divinity itself. . . . We too will be food for other generations of living things, so we might as well begin today by letting go of hoarding and entering the chain of being as food for one another."[6]

Each time we see the world this way, in terms of its enoughness, and enact our vision by insisting upon the just distribution of all goods, material and otherwise, we realize in part the Community of God, though not all of us will call it that. No matter. The point is to get not the words but the deeds right, the ones that lead to "the liberation of the whole human being and all human beings—the liberation of all oppressed dimensions, personal and social, of human life in all of the subjects of that life, without the exclusion of anyone or anything,"[7] an end entirely beyond the capabilities of either Communism or capitalism. Nothing less will do. And each of us committed to this vision must act *first*, that is, without awaiting permission from the proper authorities, guidance from leaders at the local, national, or international level, or the results of a probablistic study assessing our "realistic" chances of attaining such a prodigious goal. No one with the power to give permission or guidance is going to give it for an end designed to rob him of that very power. And our chances, I can tell right now, are nil.

The enormity of the world's messes understandably overwhelms us ordinary mortals, who may find ourselves complaining, like the middle-aged Texas woman in a recent *New York Times* interview, "All I know for sure is something drastic has got to change and somebody has got to decide where this country is going to go instead of getting up there and giving us the same old, same old."[8] Look how impersonally, how powerlessly she speaks: "something," "somebody . . . up there." Who does she think is going to do it? Obviously not herself: she just crouches while the "same old, same old" showers down from on high. God, then?

Not on your life. That's what we're here for: to make the world new. We know what to do: seek justice, love mercy, walk humbly, treat every person as though she were yourself. These are not complicated instructions. It's much harder to decipher the directions for putting together a child's tricycle than it is to understand these. Nor are the behaviors they require alien to our habits and desires. We engage in them routinely, not perforce but by preference, unlike truly alien behaviors. How many times, for instance, have you shot someone dead with an M-16? Probably nowhere near as many, whatever your military experience, as you have stroked your son's head over the years since he was born. How many times have you cheated a client, gotten high on cocaine, slept with your best friend's spouse, spat in the face of a beggar, stolen a bicycle from your neighbor's porch, swerved your car in order to hit a dog? No matter how many wicked things you've done, chances are you've done astronomically more good ones. At the personal level, within our families and communities, we tend to treat one another decently and with remarkably good humor.

A new world order will not emerge from the commitment, recently called for by the Pentagon, to "precluding the emergence of any potential future global competitor," in a repudiation of "collective internationalism" which would leave the United States without "rivals" in a "one-superpower world."[9] Talk about "same old, same old," dribbling down on our aching heads in the spent rhetoric of conquest: Hannibal, Attila the Hun, Genghis Khan, Charlemagne, William the Conqueror, Napoleon, you-know-who, the Evil Empire, and now . . . US! We know how to play mine-is-bigger-than-yours-and-can-pee-farther-too as though we were born to the game. Just take a look at George Bush—or, should he no longer be president, whoever has taken his place, since one rich white educated U.S. male essentially duplicates the next and our "two-party" system is designed to reproduce these the way Mattel spews out G.I. Joes while thwarting all challenges to their hegemony.

A *new* world order—a wholly fresh way of conceiving relatedness as inclusive and egalitarian rather than exclusive and hierarchical—requires a shift to the rhetoric of communion, in which we generally conduct our ordinary affairs already. "Would you like half my sandwich?" "May I please have a glass of water?" "I don't enjoy playing pool. Let's go to the movies instead." "I can drive you to work while your car is in the shop." "Would you like me to teach you to play the guitar?" "There's only one doughnut left. Let's flip a coin for it." "Here's my extra jacket. Wear it in good health." "Please don't let your dog trample my irises." "If we both work on it, we can finish painting the house before dark." These are commonplaces at the personal level. Why should their analogues sound weird at the global level? If we used them often enough, they wouldn't.

Such civility depends, of course, on the availability of resources. People who are starving and shivering—whether individually or as whole populations—tend to be snappish. But, as Matthew Fox points out, "It has been estimated that 'the money required to provide adequate food, water, education, health and housing for everyone in the world' would be seventeen billion dollars per year . . . the amount that the world spends on arms every two weeks."[10] The equitable distribution of goods and services would, assuredly, be a logistical nightmare, but hey, I know just the guys for the job: the Pentagon. If they've got the brains and resources to carry out "America's political and military mission in the post–cold-war era . . . to ensure that no rival superpower is allowed to emerge in Western Europe, Asia or the territory of the former Soviet Union,"[11] with a little retraining they should get the hang of international cooperation. Instead of being the world's Big Daddy, smacking bottoms and taking away allowances and grounding without telephone privileges for weeks at a time, they could become the Little Mother who bandages banged heads and mediates shouting matches and makes sure all the people at table clean their plates and get seconds if they want them.

"Get real," I can imagine a deep-throated chorus rumbling, as though such a program were hopelessly impractical. But impractical is precisely what it's not. It turns a deaf ear to idealistic pratings about *this great nation of ours* which has *made the world safe for democracy* (which I just misspelled "demoncracy" as though my fingers knew something the rest of me didn't) and seeks now to *restore the balance of trade* and *ensure a lasting peace* by deploying nonexistent weapons in space as a *deterrence to aggression* from *potential competitors*, concentrating instead on purely pragmatic provisions like *bread* and *warm pajamas* and *pencils for school*. "Utopia," a world in which such goods circulate freely is invariably labeled with a dismissive wave, as though *ou topos* meant not just "no place" but "place never to exist"; and of course as long as people act on the premise that a condition depending upon their will for fulfillment can never occur, it won't. But what I envision is not *ou topos* but *koinos topos*: the common place: the place in which God wills us to be whole: the Community of God. Enter it if you will.

WHOSE BODY?

You would think, wouldn't you, that a faith founded on the premise of incarnation—of the Word-that-speaks-all-into-being made flesh to dwell among us—would hold in certain respect, perhaps in outright reverence, the body, the very form in which the divine had elected to be housed. This is not a God captured in a cave or a calf made of molten gold. This God does not toss around thunderbolts like a child in a temper tantrum, require offerings of burnt meat or freshly excised human hearts or even ordinary fruits and vegetables, devour his own or anybody else's offspring, transform innocent maidens into cows. The tabernacle of this God is not a tent of linen and acacia wood, lit by golden lamps and perfumed with incense, which we may approach or must avoid depending on the state of our souls. The tabernacle of this God is *us*.

God chose to proclaim the real presence of divinity in our flesh as in all creation through a person "like us in all things but sin," according to the Eucharistic prayer. Since sin arises from the failure to love God and God's creation, and since the love of God is infinite, this exception seems inevitable. So, for that matter, does our sin, since it is one thing to bear the presence of God, as we do, and quite another to be God entire and infinitely capable of love, as we plainly are not; and whatever is inevitable might be held excusable. This is the good news: just as we might hope, our sins are forgiven, we are fully free to perform acts of justice and mercy and faith, and as we do so our capacity for love expands. The bad news is that the institution that appointed itself to promulgate the good news has spent most of two thousand years making us—all of us, but women especially—feel terrible for existing in precisely the form God chose for addressing us face to face.

One of the most remarkable attributes of the Jesus depicted in the Gospels is his concern with physical well-being. Even though the timing's not quite right, he transforms water into wine rather than spoil the wedding festivities. "They're hungry," he says, gazing out over the crowd gathered to hear him. "Let's feed them." And suddenly they're all munching bread and fish, plain fare, to be sure, but nourishing and plentiful and so tasty that they return looking for more. "I'm thirsty," he says to the woman at the well. "Give me a drink." The body's ills arouse his pity, and he cures the afflicted ones without condition, without even, in the case of the woman with the flow of blood, apparent intention. Even those raised from the dead get practical attention: "Eat a little something." "Take care of your mother." "Get out of those smelly rags."

The body he inhabits is similarly substantial—and similarly fragile. His conception occurs extragenitally, to be sure, but it leads to the birth of a genuine baby, one who can be wrapped up tight and tucked into a trough of hay and, on the eighth day after his birth, taken to have his foreskin ritually removed. He gets baptised in the usual way, with ordinary river water, and sets off on a ministry whose fundamental figure involves food: real bread, real wine. In his fables people are forever planting vineyards and pouring wine into skins, fishing, herding sheep or swine (of all things), sowing and reaping grain, baking, preparing and devouring feasts. He's fond of a feast himself, too fond, his critics say, at the wrong moments, and in the wrong company, among people who don't even wash their hands, for Pete's sake. His final meal is just such a feast.

He remains embodied to the end. In fact, the end is all we know for certain about the historical Jesus: "he died at the hands of the Romans as a rebel against their rule in Palestine."[1] He didn't have a choice. He was *human*, remember. When you're human, you're human all the way. No calling a halt to the condition when things gets nasty: "Enough for me. I'll be off now, thanks." When you're human, you go through a lot, some bits nicer than others, and then—always, always, one way or another—then you die.

Jesus' mutilated body was removed from the cross and hastily embalmed and entombed. Then, curiously, the body vanished. Some women went looking for it, and it simply wasn't there. Maybe, as D. H. Lawrence would have it, Jesus was taken down too soon, not dead at all. Maybe the body was stolen: body snatching is one meaning of the word "resurrection." The accounts of its disappearance were composed long afterward, of course, and maybe they're fictitious, although (I love this point) the fact "that women, barred from bearing testimony considered valid in a Jewish forum, were nevertheless remembered as being the first to witness to the fact is an important factor in considering its historical likelihood."[2] Only someone stuck with telling the truth would hinge his faith on the words of women.

Anyway, no sooner was the body gone from the tomb than it began showing up elsewhere. A stranger joined two of the bereaved disciples on their way to Emmaus, although it was not until supper that their eyes were opened, and they recognized him in the breaking of the bread. Mary Magdalene saw him, but no one believed her. Thomas required more than a gesture or a word but an actual touch for his own belief. As many as five hundred people may have seen him at one time. These could, of course, have been hysterical visions, which people have been known to share: folies à deux are perhaps more readily initiated than folies à douze and so on, but even the madness of multitudes is not implausible, as anyone who has attended a rock concert can attest. A missing body and its later apparition required explanation, and doubtless plenty of people opted for theories like theft and group lunacy, but a few did not. Instead, they proposed that the hypothetical resurrection of the dead, in which many already believed, had actually taken place, not at the end of the world but in the middle (though many surmised that the world could not long survive such a phenomenon). A really dead body—horribly, humiliatingly dead—had restored itself to life. Surely God had walked among us in its guise.

I love this story because I absolutely don't know what to make of it. Over and over I tell it to myself, briefly at least once a week, since it is recapitulated in the Mass, and in full during the Easter season, interpreting it each time as my academic training has conditioned me to do. "Don't you get bored," a

Presbyterian acquaintance once asked, "going through the same stuff week after week?" Actually, the readings, because they change over a three-year span, provide some variety, but I know what she means. I've been to old-style Masses where everyone rattled off responses so rapidly that my tongue couldn't follow, and if I had to bibble like that every week, I'd doubtless drop into spiritual catatonia. But if the words are spoken slowly, their very familiarity, freeing one from frantic searches through memory or the missal, urges reflection.

In the long run, technical details seem of little consequence. I don't know whether a dead body returned to life, or rather, I accept that it did while knowing perfectly well that it didn't: a doubling of vision which only a rationalist finds pathological. What is significant is that the person who was that body reconciled the human and the divine in a way so powerful that it has stayed with(in) us ever since. No longer could we keep God at a distance—up in the sky, at the top of a mountain, in a burning bush or a growl of thunder, anywhere but here—and regulate our relationship to him purely through obedience to an elaborate system of laws. God was here, and the law was unembellished: take care of each other. Anybody could obey it. Feminists may have coined the phrase "the personal is political," but the principle has been in place for at least two millenia: empowering persons by giving them a law they can, without recondite instruction, choose to obey is a political act. In terms of Jesus' personal safety, shifting power away from priests and governors was a dangerous idea. It still is.

Ironically but perhaps inevitably, the followers of the man who was assassinated for his anti-institutional views formed themselves quite quickly into the established Church, which was soon awash, for a variety of reasons, in a "rising tide of sexual pessimism"[3] and a general revulsion from corporeal matters persisting to this day. The attitude toward the body attributed to Jesus in the Gospels is mild by comparison, not hatred but a sometimes scandalous insouciance toward both practical details and ritual purity. True, he preaches drastic measures like plucking out an offending eye or lopping off an offending limb, but in light of his customary figuration, he seems unlikely to be advocating actual self-mutilation here, a point that medieval flagellants would have done well to remember (except that, if I understand Church practices of the day, they would have been denied access to the words of Jesus). He is certainly aware of the body's capacity for sin—that out of a person's heart comes a tangle of spiritual and physical wrongdoing—but when confronted by such a body, an adulterous woman, he places the power of refraining from sin squarely in her. Clearly he believes that, however weak the flesh may be, it need not be the ruin of us.

People who, following Jesus' counsel, don't worry about their lives, what they will eat or drink, or about their bodies, what they're going to wear, or about whatever is going to become of them, and who bear responsibility for their own right action, can't readily be controlled. Personal anxiety is a virtually essential prerequisite for control (as distinct from enslavement, which demands only brute force). And control provides one of the means whereby an institution establishes and sustains itself, else its members would tend to wander off every which way, reducing it to rubble. Personal anxiety grounds itself in the infantile body, where chills and hunger pangs threaten sheer extinction; and for this reason an institution intent upon staying around for a while does well to infantilize its members by claiming power over their bodies. If you tell people their bodies are loathsome, they'll feel sufficiently self-alienated to repudiate those bodies and quite gladly turn them and their pocketbooks, along with their spirits (which are, Platonic propaganda to the contrary, inextricably intermingled), over to you.

The Catholic Church, "the oldest institution in the Western world,"[4] owes its longevity in part to an almost perfect understanding of this principle. Since I don't believe that Jesus established the institutional Church, except inadvertently, I'm not implicating him here; nor am I referring to the Church insofar as it bears witness to the obedience and bravery with which he promulgated a revolutionary message that led to his crucifixion and thence, against all plausibility, to his resurrection, a sequence announcing the eruption of God into the historical world. But the Church exists also—perhaps primarily, in the minds of most—as a temporal establishment, and its leaders, as in any politico-legal organization structured hierarchically, have their own hegemonic interests at heart which, for politico-theological reasons, they project upon their "Lord" Jesus, Christ the "King," so that abasement becomes the correct Christian posture. A clear line divides self-chosen humility from other-imposed humiliation, however, a line that Jesus, with his gentleness toward harlots and tax collectors, clearly discerned but that his vicars on earth have sometimes had a little trouble making out through the vapors of their own self-importance.

Nowhere is this muzziness plainer than in the link between baseness and the body forged by Hellenized Christianity. Early on, as Paul's warning to the Corinthians indicates, the body was believed capable of immoral acts—idolatry, adultery, sexual perversion, theft, greed, drunkenness, revilement, robbery— but not doomed to them. "Do you not know that your body is a temple of the Holy Spirit within you, which you have from God?" Paul writes (1 Cor. 6.19). I remember misreading this passage some time ago as Paul's denial of the body's bodiness, and I think it is often construed in this way. But I see now that he actually sacralizes rather than repudiates the body: "glorify

God *in your body*" (1 Cor. 6.20, my italics). Your body, all that you have/are, is worthy to house and reveal the holy, in even its most ordinary tasks: the child's knee bandaged, the black cat fed, the lover clasped and released, the dying friend kissed goodbye.

Nevertheless, Paul himself isn't exactly crazy about the body qua body; it is not, for him, an intrinsically sound set of functions and behaviors without need of outside supervision and intervention. Those who came after him believed even more strongly that, left to its own devices and desires, which are, puzzlingly and perversely, not those of the God who created it, the body will surely run amok. The route is long and tortuous, but continuous, between Paul's admonitions and the one that has for years been tacked to one corner of my bulletin board: "All witchcraft comes from carnal Lust which is in Women insatiable." By the fifteenth century, when the *Malleus Maleficarum* guided the Church's inquisitors in their grisly extirpation of heresy, the wonder of incarnation had given way to the horror of carnality: the temple had turned into a tomb.

Not by chance are witchcraft, carnal lust, and women concatenated in the same sentence. More people may have been slaughtered during the Inquisition than during this century's Holocaust, the great preponderance of them women, and not just any women, either, but particularly those versed in medicine and midwifery. Many of the women tortured and torched during those centuries possessed surprisingly sophisticated knowledge about birth control and abortion, and the Inquisition systematically sought to exterminate them *because of that knowledge*, not because they danced naked with Satan on the heath. By this time—indeed, almost from time immemorial— the female body had become the nexus of dread, hostility, hatred, and disgust among those in power, who by definition did not wear such a body.[5] The Jesus of the Gospels appears unusually open to women as he does to other oppressed castes, speaking to them publicly, healing them and their loved ones, forgiving their sins, teaching them among his disciples, incorporating the details of their daily lives into his parables; and the very early church, before it became the Church, may have permitted women to preach and prophesy.[6] But throughout most of its history, the Church has despised and dismissed or destroyed them.

In the main, then, this has been the ecclesiastical message to the body of the faithful: *Your immortal soul, trapped in vile, loathsome, corrupt, and filthy flesh fit only to rot and be devoured by worms, has been so tainted that, upon your inevitable death, it will be doomed to eternal torment unless you atone for your sins. This, because of your nasty nature, you cannot do on your own, but fortunately for you, some of us have achieved a special relationship with God, in fact, we actually stand in for Him, He prefers us to you, and we will tell you how to do it. Maybe. But you must do exactly as we say. Exactly as we say. Exactly.* Anyone who thinks this vision of helpless human depravity overblown need only look at Middle English religious poetry or the paintings of Hieronymous Bosch in order to admire my restraint.

Oh, yes, but that was hundreds of years ago, you may say. Since then we've experienced the Renaissance and the Reformation and the Enlightenment and the death of God. Jesse Helms and friends have a bit of a thing about bodily fluids, true, but surely no one still thinks of the body categorically as a stinking cesspool of sin through which every evil seeps into the world. I wouldn't have thought so, either, but for a stunning encounter with a Dominican brother a couple of years ago. Brother Tim, visiting the Newman Center for a few days, had an Inner Healing Ministry, we were told at the end of Mass. I had by then conceived the idea for this book but was utterly helpless to begin. Several years earlier, with the help of Sister Ursula at the Newman Center, I'd achieved a breakthrough in understanding my then crumbling marriage, but she had left, alas. Perhaps Brother Tim could unstick me (my openness to such a hope captures pretty well the desperation of the non-writing writer), so I called and made an appointment to see him.

He was smaller and older and looked less bookish than I'd imagined, but he greeted me pleasantly enough and asked me to tell him about my situation. I tried to describe the difficulty I encountered in giving myself permission to write about God. I had the sense that he wasn't gripped by my problem. Instead, after a bit, he began asking me about my relationship with George. Since this had been renewed and was now flourishing, I was puzzled by his tack, but I obligingly sketched it for him. Did we have satisfactory sexual relations? In fact, we had: If books could be jumpstarted by ardent sex, I should already have poured out reams. Had we, he asked suddenly, ever had oral intercourse? Well, of course we'd had oral intercourse. Aha, there lay the trouble: the devil uses sodomy to gain access to the world, and George and I had repeatedly flung wide the gates.

With obvious satisfaction, he recounted how women hearing his message sometimes threw up for twenty minutes or more, as though spasmodic purgation were proof of the words' virtue. I wished that I could throw up, too, to cleanse my system of the poisonous misogyny and homophobia sluicing in through my ears as he expatiated raptly upon "unnatural" acts. Somehow the interview drew to a close, and after stopping in the lady chapel to light a candle for Anne, on her way home from Zaïre, I returned shakily to my house. For myself, old and experienced and resourceful, the matter wasn't grave; but the Newman Center's essential ministry is to students at the University of Arizona, in whose company I'd spent much of my life. During student years, when self-absorption and sexual anxiety are nearly overwhelming, people don't need to be told that they are the source of the world's evils: they already suspect themselves of the worst. They don't need to be directed toward picking the sores on their souls. I wanted to put my arms protectively around anyone Brother Tim had spoken to and whisper: *The world may well end if you cut down its trees and pave it over; it may well end if you permit its people to go unfed and unclothed and uneducated while you prosper. But the world will not end if you touch your genitals. The world will not end even if you touch someone else's genitals. I can think of sound reasons for choosing not to do so, but fear and disgust should not be among them. Your body is not a pesthouse, it is simply a body: who you are: part of God's creation, a small part, true, but as real and lovely as the rest. If you love every part, evil will not enter the world through you. Through Brother Tim, maybe, but not through you.*

Since Brother Tim's monomaniacal ministry is the only one I've encountered in almost a decade and a half of Catholic observance, it can't (please God) be common. But the disgust for the body, particularly the sexualized female body, which makes such a ministry even conceivable suffuses Church attitudes and practices so thoroughly as to seem inherent in, rather than imposed upon, human consciousness. The Church forces its essential premise, the incarnation of God, to detour around ordinary bodily experience, as though God wouldn't deign to put on flesh contaminated through sexual conception but insisted on an unused container, as though what's good enough for us wasn't good enough for him. Now, I like the account of the virgin birth, which isn't unique to Christianity, because it functions just as it ought: to draw attention to the miraculous change in the relationship of the human to the holy which Christ catalyzed. In fact, I'm devoted to Mary in her manifestation as La Virgen de Guadalupe, whose slightly anxious image gazes down at me as I wrench out these words. But I'm also drawn to the story of a young woman so crazy about the carpenter she's going to marry that she can't quite wait and thus finds herself "in trouble," just the way my husband's students, girls of fourteen or fifteen or sixteen, often find themselves. In the interest of humility, mightn't God have chosen just such a vessel?

Since the only accounts we have were written long after the event, I don't know whether or not Mary's hymen was intact when Jesus was conceived; but, having expelled two fully formed infants through my vagina, I'm quite certain that it wasn't by the time she wrapped him in swaddling clothes and laid him in the manger. Only a bunch of celibate men with too little useful work to perform would be likely to grow obsessed with the question, at any rate, and squander intellectual energy on it as well as on defending Joseph's concomitant virginity and explaining away Jesus' brothers and sisters. Whether or not we can reasonably point to this blessed event as a historical example of parthenogenesis isn't the point, though. The point is that the Church in history has been driven by a desperate desire to distance the divine from the human in a movement precisely diametrical to that embodied in Christ. Heaven forfend there should be blood and torn membranes at the sacred birth.

This disgust for and denial of the processes associated with its own fundamental premise accounts for much of the Church's chronic but not congenital dis-ease. Its arrogance in claiming the (often infallible) power to control the bodies of the faithful, in particular the female faithful, and thereby to snatch from them the power to choose for themselves either right action or "sin," together with the perversity of its teaching on matters like masturbation, homosexuality, celibacy, birth control, and abortion, has corrupted its relationship to God and God's people, reducing it from mediator to prurient scold. Perhaps no entity, whether individual or institution, which transforms itself from moral guide to legal guardian, thereby depriving an other of free will, can escape such corruption.

As a consequence of locating the incarnation in a preposterous matrix—a Virgin Mother—the Church's treatment of women has been especially reductive and coercive. Incapable of replicating the model as a whole, a woman must settle for one term or the other. Well, at least she has a choice. But wait: owing to the "naturally spousal predisposition of the feminine personality,"[7] whether she chooses motherhood or virginity, she is "'married' either through the sacrament of marriage or spiritually through marriage to Christ."[8] Mutatis mutandis, she winds up some guy's wife, only one way she gets labor pains, her "very physical constitution," not to mention her "psycho-physical structure," being "naturally disposed to motherhood—conception, pregnancy and giving birth—which is a consequence of the marriage union with the man,"[9] and the other way she doesn't. (If you think, by the way, that I've dredged up some quaint text for these pronouncements, take a look at the date in the endnotes.)

I'm not derogating motherhood here. I've been a mother, both biologically and nonbiologically, and on the whole I'm well pleased with the experience. Nor am I disparaging virginity/celibacy as a freely elected spiritual practice. But I feel downright queasy at having these two, and only these two, options prescribed for all women. Where is the wife who elects (for reasons of health, profession, economics, or what have you—for, that is, her own reasons) not to become a mother? Where is the woman who cannot, physically or psychologically, risk a pregnancy at this moment in her life? Where is the woman who prefers to remain single but not celibate, or, for that matter, celibate but not single? Where is the lesbian mother who prefers to avoid "the marriage union [or any other sort] with the man?" These women have been my friends, my sisters, in some instances my self. Am I to ignore them? Cajole them? Coerce them? Condemn them?

I will not. Those tasks do not belong to me, nor do they belong to any institution. With regard to "reproductive rights," that is, the autonomous power of a woman to determine whether and when her body will produce offspring, the Church fathers, as well as other patriarchs of society, have traditionally sought to arrogate that power to themselves in adopting an absolutist stance currently called "pro-life." "God's law is higher than man's law," insists the leader of the militant anti-abortion group Operation Rescue, revealing the only two operant parties in this legalistic fray, as though God and man were knights jousting over the virtue of the fair helpless maiden. But God does not pay the rent and provide the groceries, and too often no man does either. No one may rightly dissuade, much less legally block, a woman from having an abortion who is not prepared to say to her, "The life of this baby is so important to me that, if you can't provide for it yourself—never mind why—I will do so, if only you will allow it to be born," and then to make good the promise if she permits. I think it would do someone like Cardinal Ratzinger a world of good to spend eighteen years rearing a child (though what it would do to the child worries me considerably).

For myself, I belong to that enormous group, very likely a majority, in fact, who are both pro-choice and anti-abortion. The experience of two pregnancies, both planned, has persuaded me that life is present, however primitively and potentially, from conception; and I was fortunate, as many women are not, that such life in no way threatened my own. Although I believe that reproductive questions lie so radically in the realm of private conscience that they ought to remain outside the legal arena altogether, they often require personal consultation. In general, if a woman asked my counsel, I would not recommend abortion. "God came to us this way," I would probably tell her. "God comes again and again." With enough effort and support, one can always create space for a little more God in one's life.

But what if the one who came to me was not a woman in the abstract but my young friend Bonnie, seeking not just counsel but comfort in the wake of "a contraceptive failure," she tells me breathlessly over the telephone. Bonnie has cerebral palsy, and her fiancé, Bill, lost both legs in a motorcycle accident. Although their distraught parents, certain that they can't take care of themselves, let alone a child, assume that abortion is imperative, she can count on my angle of vision, as the family's resident cripple and Catholic, to lie along a different slant. I can hear in her voice how desperately she and Bill yearn for this baby, and I believe that, with physical assistance, they can become excellent parents. But I also understand that the powerful medication she currently takes can cause severe genetic damage.

"I know you don't want this abortion," I tell her. "I don't blame you. But I agree with the doctors that you should go ahead with it. Then get off the drug and start again fresh, on purpose, making a healthy baby. The details will work themselves out." I love Bonnie, Bonnie herself, in all her complicated being. That is my task. Not to scream in her face, smear her with spittle and blood, call her up in the dead of night and tell her she's a baby-killer. Especially not just now, when her distress is so great. She needs to make a monumental and by no means clear-cut moral decision, which no one can do well under duress. My task—the task of every human creature in relation to every other—is neither to condone nor to condemn but simply to encourage: to put heart in.

Such a task is not supported by any system—call it Supreme Court, call it Natural Law, call it Necessity—that teaches a woman to despise her body, its delights, its accidents, and to relinquish responsibility for it to a higher institutional power. On the contrary, institutions, which must retain power in order to remain in place, systematically subvert personal responsibility, replacing it with a set of legal constraints and consequences, the more elaborate and thus inescapably transgressible the better, since really no law serves its purpose unless it has ample opportunity to show its "teeth." For this reason, the Church—by which I mean not the Body of Christ made up of faithful persons, who tend toward self-regulation, but the administrative hierarchy, which tends through legalism toward self-aggrandizement—may be wholly incapable of providing reliable moral education. If it did lead us out of our childish fearfulness and dependency, sustain our efforts at choosing wisely and acting well, and celebrate our successes rather than condemn our inevitable failures, in the long run what would we need it for? No institution sanctions its own obsolescence.

"A morally viable Church" may thus be more of an oxymoron than "a Catholic feminist." Enfeebled by actions and attitudes that border on the mad, the Church may have to be written off as a loss to anything but itself. Like a snake swallowing its tail, it persists in denying priesthood to women and married men while the drop in vocations leaves parish after parish unguided, defrocking gay priests who affirm their celibacy while it protects priests who sexually abuse children, simultaneously exterminating some of its own people through AIDS and condemning others to insupportably large families rather than permitting the use of condoms.

Meantime, the other church—the one meant by the phrase "we are the church"—prospers, an interactive (but not necessarily, I'm afraid, meliorative) process rather than the "institution" it is commonly taken to be, having nothing to do with standing stone-still and everything to do with bending, dancing, running around in circles, collapsing in convulsions (often enough of laughter), leaping up, reaching out, recoiling, singing and weeping at the same time. Hell looms small in this church, since it doesn't depend on dread for its power. This church incorporates people who may choose abstinence in various forms but do not permit it to be forced on them; who, regardless of gender, break bread, pour wine, and feed one another; who recognize the goodness of God in their creation as homosexuals; who make love safely to consenting partners; who prevent the conception of children they cannot care for and even, after deep reflection, terminate pregnancies; who forgive themselves and one another after the manner of the man they follow: "Neither do I condemn you; go, and do not sin again."

The members of this church know themselves to be, in the words of a nun describing the lay ministers she trains, "like God with skin on."[10] I carry a lovely picture—and it is purely imaginal, since I wasn't there—of my husband after we'd had sexual intercourse for the first time (by dim lamplight on a narrow day bed in a room papered with gold leaf, I know, I was there for that part). When he got back to his parents' house and undressed, he told me later, he stared for a long time at his body in the mirror, amazed and jubilant; and I have always treasured the image of this rapt figure barely into manhood, all bones and pale skin and black curly hair, loving himself for loving me. Similarly set in front of a mirror, the church members I have in mind may roll their eyes and grimace, dab a little cream on the crow's feet, and vow to eat fewer chocolates and more carrots, but they won't shudder and turn away in revulsion. *This is not the devil's work,* they'll say. *Nor is it Church property. This is my body. For it I am answerable only to the God I am blessed to bear in it.*

LAST THINGS

Is God's love but the last and most mysterious word for death?

—Robert Penn Warren, "Heart of the Backlog"

T here's just no point in writing this book," I say to my husband. "Some other woman has done it already." We are eating one of the quickie meals he can throw together when he gets home from school at eight, fettuccine with a very expensive sauce marketed by Paul Newman, who should, in view of the number of green peppers he's used, have stuck to acting. My fettuccine is mounded on a yellow plastic plate with a rolled rim so that my floppy hand won't shove the chopped-up bits all over the table. "Only hers is called *Virgin Time.* 'A personal exploration of Roman Catholic spirituality,' her biographical note in this week's *Book Review* said."

Today I have written only one paragraph, and that a stupid one. As I left my studio, I knocked my computer glasses and a pile of old letters, bundled chronologically, onto the floor, and since I can no longer get down there, except accidentally and irreversibly, I'll have to ask George to pick them up. The housekeeper had left the dog outside on his line, and he sat without a flinch but with many a sigh and roll of eye while I fumbled and tugged at the clasp. The House and Senate both stand ready to increase funding for Star Wars, MacNeil/Lehrer informed me, and the hole in the ozone layer is significantly larger than scientists have previously estimated. Absorbed by the irony of installing a destructive umbrella even as you rip the protective one away, as though it matters whether you get fried to a crisp by a bomb or by the sun, I backed my scooter into the metal bowl, battered already into an oval during earlier lapses of attention, and slopped the dog's water all over. "Aaaaah," I howled. "Let me out of here. God, let me out of here!" But I'm still here, poking at the green peppers Paul Newman used too many of. And some other woman has written my book, only her time is virginal whereas mine is ordinary.

"That's her book," George says. He is eating his fettucine from a flat black octagonal plate, twining the long strands deftly around his fork, and his tone is reasonable. "You're writing your book. Some people might want to read them both."

"Oh no they won't. They'll want to read hers. She's a certified genius. Really. A MacArthur Fellow. I'm just a frivolous writer, inconsequential."

"That's not what those letters you get say. Those people take you seriously."

"Ha, what do they know? They're undiscriminating, tasteless—"

"—a bunch of boobies," he finishes for me. "The kind of club you wouldn't be caught dead joining—"

"—if they'd have me for a member." I can't keep up my petulance a moment longer. I have to giggle.

He's done it again. He's entered, with perfect sobriety, into my mood of fantastic despair, helping me spin it out to its inevitably ludicrous end. In more than thirty years, I don't think he's ever ridiculed me. But he laughs companionably when I finally reach the point of hooting at myself. Then he makes me a cup of raspberry-flavored coffee, stretches my contracted muscles while we watch the late news, pulls off my skirt and jersey, lowers me onto the bed where the black cat waits, the tip of her tail flicking, to curl into the crook of my knee, and lies down beside us.

"How did you *do* that?" I ask him in the dark.

"Huh?" Already he's more asleep than awake. "Do what?"

"You know, make me laugh, really laugh, when I was feeling so terrible."

"Oh, a Fan Club for Boobies, I think it was." His voice trails off. "I did it with a Fan Club for Boobies."

I could not have imagined a single detail of this quite ordinary evening, except possibly the black cat, and certainly not the easy intimacy pervading it, during those virginal days when I dreamed of becoming George's wife. Similarly, now I can not imagine how I can live without this man. And should not, actuarially speaking, have to do so for years and years to come. He's fifty-one, almost thirty years younger than his father was when he died, nowhere near retirement and the delights we've watched it bring to our parents, aunts and uncles, older friends. That mole on his upper arm shouldn't have turned black and bubbly, and if it did, the doctors should have cut it all away. They said so: a ninety-five percent chance that the melanoma would never recur. Not in a lymph node. Not then in his belly. He should not be getting ready to die and leave me.

But if he must, then I should be able to look forward, however unhappily, to a widowhood like that of our friends whose husbands have died prematurely. I'm forty-nine, too old and self-willed for romance or remarriage but not for friendship. Tucson is home, with George or without, but I might look for a visiting position at a college in a place I've never been, just for the adventure of it, might try living in England for a bit, a stone cottage in Upper Slaughter or Coln Rogers or even Moreton-in-Marsh, until the weather drove me buggy, or spend a year in a Catholic Worker house of hospitality. My parents, fit and alert, still live in their own home and play golf several times a week. Surely I should not already be checking on Medicare benefits and looking at retirement communities that offer custodial care for them, much less myself.

Ah well, what happens happens, without regard for propriety. The main consequence of falling a little further than most outside the margins of the actuarial charts, apart from a sort of wry outrage, is the loneliness felt by anybody whose life unfolds out of sync with general social patterns. I find it increasingly difficult to communicate with my peers, who are still embarking on new jobs, new love affairs, new books, even new babies; yet I lack the life experience of friends in their seventies and eighties who are, like us, confronting disability and death. Without clear models, I feel confused, disoriented. I also feel a little embarrassed, as though with these inopportune illnesses we're behaving rather badly. We're abandoning George's mother, who, though in robust health, grows increasingly dependent and querulous and will doubtless require more and more looking after in the years to come. We're deserting our children without giving them all time to produce the grandchildren we'd surely make fools of ourselves over, and who knows how they'll muddle through without our sage grandparently supervision.

One possible response to the scandal of our situation—and it's one I've found commonly recommended—is to think as little as possible about what's happening. Keep yourself busy, people say: join a bridge club, watch the soaps, go out with friends, plant a garden, give cocktail parties or Sunday brunches, campaign for a political candidate, learn a new language, take up yoga or knitting or ceramics. Since I'm dogged by fatigue and no longer drive, some of these suggestions are more practical than others, but that's not the point. The rationale behind them—that comfort and cheer depend on distraction, not contemplation, that only by denying some elements of one's life can one render that life supportable—repels me. And it leads, oddly, to more self-pity than I care to feel, since one is bound to feel sorry for oneself if one believes one's circumstances too ghastly to bear scrutiny. The life left after such censoring seems to me crippled and constrained.

An alternative response is to go all out with whatever you get handed, thinking about it like mad. I don't in the least mean dwelling on sorrows or reveling in misery, which would only be a kind of flip side of distraction, every bit as disabling and even more painful (unless you really, really hate bridge or Chinese grammar or what have you). I mean bringing the whole of life to consciousness, on the premise that what you deny knowing can hurt you. Some years ago, the youthful, energetic editor of *Remembering the Bone House* expressed high hopes for the book. "But Lisa," I cautioned her, "this isn't *Everything I Needed To Know I Learned in Kindergarten*. The subtext here is that we are all going to die, and that that's all right. It's not a message that will attract readers in droves." Alas for the sales figures, I was right, but I'm not sorry I wrote as I did. Taught through intimate relations with disability and death that life, though lugubrious enough, is even more ludicrous and that no one develops fully until she can play and mourn in balance, I had to risk a messenger's death then and still must do: We *are* all going to die. And it *is* all right.

"Are you afraid of death?" my therapist asks me one afternoon when I've dragged yet another life crisis into his bright corner office overlooking the University of Arizona campus. I sometimes tease Ken that, in the nearly twenty years we've worked together, I've provided him a solid education in the developmental stages of an educated, middle-class, Anglo-American family. At our first meeting, I was a graduate student, the mother of young children, newly diagnosed with a chronic, incurable, but not necessarily terminal degenerative disease. Together and separately, George and I have offered him suicide attempts, marital infidelities, doctoral examinations, disputes over child-rearing, bouts of cancer, breakdowns in communication, sexual dysfunction, and an occasional Greek salad with anchovies at our favorite taverna.

"No, not of death," I say to him. "Not of being dead, that is. But of dying, yes, I'm very afraid of the process." Ken can't cure me of my fear, I know, but in permitting me to articulate it, he helps ready me to work on it. The tongues of most people I know trip in their haste to forbid the subject of death. *Oh, you don't need to think about that now,* they gibber, *not for years and years, don't be so gloomy, it's not good for you, wear bright colors and go see a Steve Martin movie.* I tend to dress in earth tones (the kind that make my daughter sigh, "Bo-ring"); Steve Martin is about the only comic actor I can bear to watch; and I don't think either of those facts is going to increase or decrease by one cubit the span of my life. Nor do I think that a magic moment will arrive when the death I am not yet permitted to ponder will suddenly become suitable for speculation. Misreadings of writers like

Norman Cousins and Bernie Siegel have led to a kind of terror-
ism of cheerfulness, which blames people for getting sick and
dying because they failed to be jolly enough to disarm the grim
reaper. An authentically blithe spirit, studies suggest, really can
enhance the immune system, which may then fight off disease
and thus even prolong life, but people can't grin their way out
of death any more than they can grump their way into it. It will
come when it will come. Repressing all recognition of it, however, constricts the very life one seeks to augment. Thoughts of
death darken one's spirit, to be sure, but they also deepen it.

Ken is one of the rare people who can, quite calmly and
with some amusement, permit such an exploration to go on.
We've just been laughing about a conversation George and I
had not long before, in which, when I mentioned envisioning
George at my bedside when I died, he protested, "But I imagine
you at *my* side when *I* die." *Oh dear*, I thought at the time, *this is
not going to work out to everyone's satisfaction.* Later, when I tell the
same story to the nurse case manager who is helping me prepare
to live alone, and whose four years working with Hospice have
given her Ken's sort of tranquility and humor, she says, "But I'm
not so sure." I frown a little, puzzled, and she adds, "He may
come back for you. I've seen a lot of people die, and they don't
usually die alone." Maybe she's right. I don't believe in ghosts,
but George's being is so incorporated into my own, perhaps into
my very cells, that I can well imagine reconstituting his presence as I follow him into death.

"What do you think death is?" Ken asks me now. "What's it
like?" He sounds not merely clinical but curious, and it occurs
to me that, unlike the personal pecadillos I've brought to him in
the past, this is one of the few subjects that, transcending the
boundaries of nation, race, class, gender, and religion which
crisscross and fragment the human population, holds universal
interest and brooks no disbelief. That is, you may disbelieve

whatever you like *about* death, but you cannot disbelieve *in* death. It is our only absolute. If anything, it deserves more recognition and reflection than we give it, not less.

The religious faith of many people I know prepares them to give ready answers to questions like Ken's, but mine does not, even though I profess every week to believe in "the resurrection of the dead and the life of the world to come." I figure it's all right to repeat these words, a venial lie, anyway, since I might well believe them if I had any idea what they meant and maybe sheer reiteration will force them to yield up their meaning one day. This—both the creed and my hopes for it—constitutes what is called wishful thinking, which has for some reason gotten a bad name but which is really the only way we can be cajoled to throw ourselves forward into one unknown moment after another. Take it from me, a chronic depressive, who has from time to time found herself incapable of thinking wishfully. By this measure enabled to make up the story of our lives as we go along, we must perforce account for death—as either The End or not The End—as well.

At my father's death when I was four and a half, he ascended into heaven. I was told so, and I believed it just as seriously as George believed, at about the same age, that the cows in Vermont grew legs longer on one side of their bodies than on the other so as to negotiate the steep hillsides without tumbling down. Perhaps because heaven is, according to David Byrne of Talking Heads, a place where nothing ever happens, I don't recall ever forming an image of it, winged angels with harps and streets paved with gold belonging to some other fiction, nothing to do with Daddy. Eventually, I must have learned about hell, since it's mentioned in the Bible, which I read straight through when I was thirteen (a project ideally suited to such an age though not recommended for anyone much older), but I could imagine it even less, since I didn't know anybody there.

Some people I know have kept the kind of naïveté that permits them to envision their loved ones ensconced in paradise, doing there whatever they most loved to do here, and to anticipate a glad reunion, but that way seems closed to me.

Despite being a scientific booby, I understand hazily that when I die, the myriad biological functions that we lump loosely together as life will cease, and that will be the end of me. That is, since the "I" that I conceive myself to be is constituted by complex biochemical events played out in a discrete organism, when those stop, my subjectivity terminates, and whatever happens next will not be experienced in any way that I can currently comprehend. I don't believe there's any personal residue: no separable soul, no homunculus that slips from my mouth on my last breath, leaving my corpse infinitesimally lighter as it flits upward into bliss. What survives, having nothing to do with the Nancy Mairs you and I know, will be utterly unfathomable by human means.

And yet none of us can leave the matter alone. What then? we want to know. What now? What next? To give tongue to our radical uncertainty, we resort to figuration from our ordinary lives, according to the cultural patterns prepared for us. Take this somber and poignant image, which could have been conceived only by a man from a sparsely populated, densely wooded country in a northern clime, in this case the Venerable Bede:

> this present life of people on earth, compared with that time which is unknown to us, is as though you were sitting at a feast with your nobles and attendants in wintertime, the fire lit and your hall warmed, while it rained and snowed and stormed outside; a sparrow came and flew quickly through that house, came in through one door, went out through the other. Lo, while inside he is not harmed by the winter's storm, but that

least time is the blink of an eye, for he soon from winter into winter comes again. Thus does this human life appear a little while; what goes before or what follows after, we do not know.[1]

How exquisite that swift traverse of firelight and warmth and the carousing of friends between dark and dark: all that we know.

I am going where "I" am not, a state for which the impenetrability of darkness seems the aptest metaphor. Having spent my whole life in a post-Einsteinian universe, however, I believe firmly in everlasting existence at the most essential level, and I love to think of it: all my colorful, charming quarks dancing outward into vastness. "After I'm dead, look out into the Milky Way," I say to Ken. "There I'll be."

Planning for death, even with the support of therapists and nurses who do not strive to distract you, is decidedly more difficult than planning for any of life's other major events. We are creatures who adore the sense of control we achieve through giving advice. Perhaps that's why we developed language in the first place, purely so as to have the means for cautioning and directing each other where to go to college, which career to choose, who to marry, what to wear at the wedding, how to get pregnant, when to toilet train, whether or not to divorce. We're all old hands at something about which we can pass on our expertise. Except for death, at which, like birth, we get a single shot, with no opportunity to communicate our newly acquired competence. "Here, it's easy," we never get a chance to say, "I've done it a thousand times, watch me!" In addition to a lack of qualified personnel to talk us through the event, we're hampered by various resistances, our own, of course, but others' as well, which suggest that we oughtn't to die at all but, if we must, we ought at least to keep decently composed and pretend something else—much nicer—is happening.

The combination of ineptitude and resistance can create a muddle, with the dier (yes, there is such a word, though the unaccustomed agency it implies is startling) made, through inexperience, to feel stupid and clumsy; the livers, through denial or uncertainty, to suffer betrayal, anger, guilt, and panic in various measures; and everybody to appear menacingly out of control. Although sudden death, like my father's at twenty-eight, can't always be anticipated, age or illness warns many of us. The last time George saw his father, at eighty, Dad was ready to talk about his death; at the first mention of it, however, Mum would run from the room weeping, so no preparations could be made. The result, when Dad died a month later, was an emotional and practical uproar.

Perhaps because of my father's death, my family had responded very differently when my grandmother, in her late sixties, learned she had a massive abdominal aneurism. The condition, inoperable in those days, set a time bomb, which went off four years later. In the interim, persuaded by her children that she should relish her well-deserved retirement from her job as a bank teller, she budgeted her meager funds for the travel she had longed for: Florida, Bermuda, and finally Germany, which her parents had left before her birth in the 1890s. A thoroughly pragmatic and good-humored woman, she also spoke with us, from time to time, about the arrangements for her death: who was to have the amethysts, what hymns she'd like sung at her memorial service. She approved of the plots she and my parents had bought at the top of the Enon cemetery overlooking the golf course, where she could keep an eye on my stepfather, and insisted on being buried before any church service so that we would focus not on her casket but on her memory. Her death came abruptly and was, as even such a well laid out event will be, a shock. But thanks to her instructions she remained—just around the corner, upstairs while we were down, in some other room—to guide us through it.

Granna's manner, though sometimes solemn, was not morbid. You don't have to want death in order to prepare for it. Nor are your preparations "asking for it." There's something ghoulish about such superstitions, a relinquishing of power to death as though it were a malevolent entity that must be fought off instead of an indispensable stage of maturation. One of the advantages of adopting a religious rather than a secular heuristic is that death can never, even inadvertently, be scanted. As a Catholic, I am confronted week after week by a body "given up" for me, for my benefit, my liberation, and I know that it was given up to death, as mine will be. I may resist but I may not neglect this necessary end. My life takes its whole meaning— all its sweetness as well as all its terrors—from it.

But the death for which I must plan now appears to be George's, not my own. I don't see why this should be. If *I* were in charge, I would give the melanoma to the one already ruined by multiple sclerosis and leave the healthy one unharmed. It's probably a good thing I'm not in charge, however, since every time a motorist cuts me off in traffic I hurl imprecations—"Die! Die, you rude dog!"—and the highways would be perpetually littered with corpses. No one, in this sense, is in charge. That is, no one handed George melanoma and me MS, with the idea, no doubt, of spreading the goods around. That Which Will Be (which I generally call God but others may call fate or chaos or nothing at all) doesn't work that way. For some reason, people assume that belief in God compels belief that God causes dreadful events to befall one; a college friend was convinced that God punished her sins (which, since she was a pale, timid girl, can't have been many) by sending her bad bridge hands. Admittedly, *I* would cause dreadful events to befall you, especially if you squeezed into the lane six inches in front of my radiator grille, and I wouldn't put it past you to cause dreadful events to befall me, but God is another order of being, upon whom we would do well not to project our nastier predilections.

As far as my cramped and fragile human capacities can determine, George has melanoma, and I do not, for absolutely no reason at all. In natural terms, a complex of poorly understood genetic and environmental mechanisms evidently triggers the growth of aberrant cells that mass themselves into the black tumors that give this cancer its name; but no informing genius sets it in motion to bring about this end. What lacks reason does not necessarily lack purpose, however. I'm not being semantically tricky here. I simply mean that any process, however impersonal and incomprehensible its origins, can function at the personal level to rouse and intensify consciousness of itself and its significances. Although, during the sweet borrowed time of the remission that currently blesses us, the details of our life are as ordinary as ever—a haircut for the corgi and new pads for the coolers in April's sudden heat—we now occupy the world in an entirely new way.

Coming to death, then, is a kind of conversion experience, a turning away from old angers and infidelities, a turning toward this moment, and this moment, and this one, and this. Death has moved into our household—not a welcome guest, oh, no, our courtesy doesn't extend that far, though for now a docile one—and its presence, far from rendering us morose, has made us spiritually alert and vigorous. One might almost say we *need* death in order to live this fully. The Buddhist Monk Thich Nhat Hanh writes,

> When we have a compost bin filled with organic material which is decomposing and smelly, we know that we can trans-

form the waste into beautiful flowers. At first, we may see the compost and the flowers as opposite, but when we look deeply, we see that the flowers already exist in the compost, and the compost already exists in the flowers. It only takes a couple of weeks for a flower to decompose. When a good organic gardener looks into her compost, she can see that, and she does not feel sad or disgusted. Instead she values the rotting material and does not discriminate against it. It takes only a few months for the compost to give birth to flowers.[2]

Preparing for death entails the gardener's mindfulness, not hurrying the rot, not forcing the bloom, above all not missing an instant of the transmutation.

George has a compost heap, out under the privet near where the doddering beagle and the comic terrier are buried; he feeds it morning and night. Last week he brought in from the porch an amaryllis, which burst into pentecostal flame in the center of the living room. Today the blossoms are a little crinkled around the edges, and the fleshy stalk is beginning to list. I know where it's headed, one morning quite soon. The bulb won't bloom for another year. Will George see those flowers? Do I want to know?

Remissions end. We do what we can to be ready. Sometimes it's hard to refrain from doing too much, like the time last year we almost sold our beloved elderly house and moved into a new little townhouse, until we discovered that George wanted a smaller place for me to get around in and I wanted one easier for him to maintain and we'd almost created our own version of O. Henry's "Gift of the Magi." More sensibly, we've protected ourselves against the use of life-prolonging but not life-enhancing devices like ventilators and tube feeding by putting living wills in the hands of doctor, lawyer, children. We've sought financial advice. We've joined the Tucson Memorial

Society. Most important, we found (in the Hemlock Society newsletter, of all places) a support group called Living with Cancer, which meets Monday mornings at a nearby Methodist church. Among these friends I've learned that—contrary to my belief that once cancer had metastasized, one spent whatever time one had left dying, more or less quickly, in a constant battle against pain—one may live, with ferocity and humor, right to the end and then be launched, like a world traveler aboard the Queen Mary in some old film, by a throng waving handkerchiefs and blowing kisses and straining their eyes till the ship slides over the horizon.

"Oh, look at those! Aren't they wonderful!" George says, stopping by a display of Chinese porcelain jars, all sizes and shapes, inexpensive but painted with charming designs in blue and white. "Put me in one of those!" He wants to be cremated, he has told me, and his ashes scattered out at Desert House of Prayer, the Redemptorist retreat in the Tucson Mountains. But an elderly friend whose husband died last summer told us she planned to keep a few of his ashes in just such a jar—"so I can talk to him and tell him how mad I am at him for dying and leaving me!"—and I was taken with the idea. It's too soon to buy one now. At least, we don't stop and pick one out, and we've learned that we'll do things when the time feels right. One day, with him or by myself, I suppose I'll choose: one with bearded irises like those he grows in a whiskey barrel, I hope, or a hummingbird like the ones who shriek and scold at our back door.

At the time we discovered the third recurrence of George's melanoma, in December 1990, his oncologist, who is also my primary-care physician, pulled my chart and noted: "Patient is devastated." When I came upon this while examining my records a few months later, I was both touched that Dr. Jackson had taken the trouble and struck by the accuracy of his language. *Devastated* was precisely how I felt: laid waste: my soul stunned and silent in a burnt-out sunless landscape. Although already ravaged by the fact that, a few weeks beforehand, he had become impotent, and shortly after that had told me about his long affair with Sandra, depriving me through this sequence of the sexual reassurance I badly needed, in the face of his illness I didn't care about those trivialities. As far as I was concerned, he didn't ever have to have an erection again, and he could have as many extramarital affairs as he liked (the fact that one of those conditions very likely precluded the other escaped my distracted notice), JUST AS LONG AS HE DIDN'T DIE.

While he was still in hospital recovering (maybe) from the massive infection caused by weeks of seepage from his perforated bowel and the removal of the offending tumor, Anne took me for my annual neurological checkup. "I'm going to ask you a question I know you can't answer," I said to my neurologist, a pale, slender, silent woman chosen, at Dr. Jackson's recommendation, precisely because she can accept such questions without going into a dither of defense and denial. "But it haunts me, so I'm going to ask it anyway. How long is this going to take?"

"I'm not much of a prognosticator, I'll warn you," she said. "I've got a patient with a brain tumor I thought had six to nine months. It's been three years and he's still working full time. But . . . a dozen years?" She shrugged. "After that, a dozen more?"

I was dumbstruck. A few months later, when Dr. Jackson told me that, except for MS, I was in fine shape, I could laugh, "This is not good news," knowing he'd accept my meaning. But in the first desolate weeks of George's relapse, my emotional tone was even flabbier than my muscle tone. Until this point, I'd thought that my quickening deterioration in the last few years would result in death before very long. Now I faced a decade, maybe more, helpless and alone. Because MS is a disease of the white and not the grey matter (Hercule Poirot's "little grey cells"), the worst of my situation, according to my neurologist, was likely to be the eventual confinement of an intact consciousness in a body incapable of carrying out any voluntary functions at all.

George's remission, brought on by months of chemotherapy followed by daily biotherapy and maybe a miracle thrown in for good measure, has ameliorated my dismay for now. But it is a reprieve, I know, not a release. This would be true even if he never produced another melanoma cell but lived out his full span of years in perfect health. Once you know death's proximity, you cannot unknow it again. This is knowledge to which we all must come at our own times and in our own ways, and a lot of people put it off until the very last minute, but in their denial they may be cheating themselves. The extraordinary benefit of death, one unrecognized in the secular world, lies in its redemptive quality. Horribly constrained in a body that can no longer roll over in bed reliably, much less be trusted to arise and get to the toilet before the flood, I have never felt freer to cherish and celebrate my husband and my children and the smelly old man who comes on his trash-picking rounds to take away my aluminum cans and even (please God, one day soon) Jesse Helms.

Yet I wonder whether, when George dies, I will fall into despair and kill myself. Although my history of emotional illness makes this not merely idle speculation, under medication I don't seem to suffer more than ordinary situational depression. If I decide not to live on alone, I will have to take my own life deliberately. But is even rational suicide an option? I have freely elected a faith that emphasizes the sanctity of life (traditionally, human life, but the Church has finally begun to toss in irises and hummingbirds as well) and condemns self-murder. In fact, the only time I've ever made a private confession followed my last suicide attempt; having acknowledged and been absolved of that sin, I have refused it thereafter. Since I don't believe in hell, my refusal can't be motivated by dread of eternal damnation. What then?

"I'm not sure"—I've been thinking out loud about suicide to Anne, who was present for my neurologist's life sentence—"but I think maybe I'm supposed to see this through to the end."

"Are you saying," she asks with the little grimace, part perplexity, part disapproval, with which she greets my more metaphysical maunderings, "that you're supposed to *suffer?*" The body on the cross in most Catholic churches is the crucified rather than the risen Christ, and Catholic iconography throughout history has displayed a morbid relish for lacerated brows, bloody hearts, flayed skins, and weeping mothers with dead bodies draped across their laps. An outsider could easily conclude that suffering is a desirable and meritorious state, especially since plenty of insiders make the same mistake.

"No, I don't. I may suffer, probably I will, but I don't think I'm *supposed* to. I'm just saying maybe I need to have the whole experience, not cut it off. Of course, if I did cut it off, then that would become the whole experience. But I'm not sure it would mean the same."

I very nearly did cut it off, as Anne painfully knows, and if I had, I'd have missed many of the most satisfying bits. I would never have seen her graduate from high school and then from Smith, watched her bound down a forest path to keep up with the group of Zaïrian fish farmers whose pond she had come to inspect, gazed enraptured as she marched herself down the brick walk of the Tucson Botanical Gardens, pausing to kiss her father and me, straight into marriage with Eric. I also wouldn't have won the Western States Book Award and published *In All the Rooms of the Yellow House,* gotten my doctorate, taught at

UCLA, written *Plaintext* and *Remembering the Bone House* and *Carnal Acts* and (yes, it's almost done) *Ordinary Time*, turned into a shameless Anglophile the instant the British Airways DC-10 dropped out of the clouds directly above an estate that could have been Brideshead. I would never have tasted scones with clotted cream. I would never have tasted bat.

Although the world would hardly be a poorer place without these ordinary events, I feed on their memory gratefully now that my revels are, if not quite ended, at least winding down. Realistically speaking, the future promises more afflictions than delights, less clotted cream than bat, you might say, though actually bat wasn't so bad. I am as afraid as ever of loss and pain. Still, something tells me—I don't know what, I can't explain what, it's just a feeling I have in my bones—that I'm supposed to stay for it all.

NOTES

Introit

1. Rosemary Radford Ruether, *Disputed Questions: On Being a Christian* (Maryknoll, N.Y.: Orbis Books, 1989), p. 27.

2. Mary G. Mason, "The Other Voice: Autobiographies of Women Writers," in *Autobiography: Essays Theoretical and Critical,* ed. James Olney (Princeton, N.J.: Princeton University Press, 1980), pp. 211, 231.

3. Nathaniel Hawthorne, "Endicott and the Red Cross," in *Tales and Sketches* (New York: Literary Classics of the United States, Inc., 1982), p. 543.

4. My use of the feminine personal pronoun whenever I'm not referring to the Father God of Christian tradition represents one such choice.

Here: Grace

1. Uta Ranke-Heinemann, *Eunuchs for the Kingdom of Heaven: Women, Sexuality and the Catholic Church,* trans. Peter Heinegg (New York: Doubleday, 1990), p. 35.

In Which I Am Not Struck Blind

1. Leonardo Boff, *Faith on the Edge: Religion and Marginalized Existence,* trans. Robert R. Barr (New York: Harper & Row, 1989), p. 39.

2. New York Times, February 28, 1990.

3. Mary G. Mason, "The Other Voice," p. 210.

Dis/Re/Com/Union

1. Louis Laravoire Morrow, *My Catholic Faith* (Kenosha, Wisc.: My Mission House, 1963), p. 57.

2. Ibid., p. 354.

3. John Paul II, *On the Dignity and Vocation of Women,* Apostolic Letter,

August 15, 1988, pp. 92, 94.

4. Philip Slater, *The Pursuit of Loneliness*, 3d ed. (Boston: Beacon Press, 1990).

Room for One More

1. Lois W. Banner, *In Full Flower: Aging Women, Power, and Sexuality* (New York: Knopf, 1992), p. 127.

From My House to Mary's House

1. Boff, *Faith on the Edge*, p. 83.

God's Will

1. Leonardo Boff, *Faith on the Edge: Religion and Marginalized Existence,* tr. Robert R. Barr (New York: Harper & Row, 1989), p. 83.

2. Ibid., p. 4.

3. Ibid., p. 36.

4. Philip Allott, *Eunomia: New Order for a New World* (Oxford: Oxford University Press, 1990), pp. 386–87.

5. Boff, *Faith on the Edge*, p. 7.

6. Matthew Fox, *Creation Spirituality: Liberating Gifts for the Peoples of the Earth* (San Francisco: Harper, 1991), p. 51.

7. Boff, *Faith on the Edge*, p. 59.

8. Robert Suro, "Texas Town Sees the Race as Remote," *New York Times*, March 8, 1992, p. 14.

9. Patrick Tyler, "U.S. Strategy Plan Calls for Insuring No Rivals Develop," *New York Times*, March 8, 1992, section 1, pp. 1, 4. In response to public outcry, this stance was modified slightly in favor of international cooperation; but as the more recent Earth Summit made plain, what the United States really understands about international cooperation wouldn't fill a spotted owl's nest, if one is left.

10. Matthew Fox, *Original Blessing* (Santa Fe, N.M.: Bear & Company, 1983), p. 14.

11. Tyler, "U.S. Strategy Plan," p. 1.

Whose Body?

1. Bruce Vawter, *This Man Jesus* (Garden City, N.Y.: Doubleday, 1973), p. 56.

2. Ibid., p. 36.

3. Uta Ranke-Heinemann, *Eunuchs for the Kingdom of Heaven, The Body and Society: Men, Women, and Sexual Renunciation in Early Christianity* (New York: Columbia University Press, 1988), provide excellent, detailed histories of this process.

4. Thomas Bokenkotter, *A Concise History of the Catholic Church*, rev. ed. (Garden City, NY: Doubleday/Image, 1979), p. 11.

5. Feminist scholars who have studied and written in depth about the Church's misogynistic practices include Mary Daly and Uta Ranke-Heineman.

6. The works of Elisabeth Schüssler Fiorenza contain a wealth of information on these points.

7. John Paul II, *On the Dignity and Vocation of Women*, Apostolic Letter, August 15, 1988, p. 78.

8. Ibid., p. 81.

9. Ibid., p. 68.

10. Sister Mary Robinson, quoted in *National Catholic Reporter*, January 17, 1992.

Last Things

1. "The Conversion of King Eadwine," from the Old English translation of Bede's *Historia Ecclesiastica Gentus Anglorum*, in *Bright's Old English Grammar and Reader*, 3d ed., Frederic G. Cassidy and Richard N. Ringler, eds. (New York: Holt, Rinehart and Winston, 1971), pp. 118–120. This translation isn't so hot, but I haven't studied Old English since before I became a Catholic. In fact, now that I think of it, studying Old English doubtless helped Catholicize me.

2. Thich Nhat Hanh, "Peace Is Every Step," *Parabola* (Winter 1991): 75–76.

RESOURCES

For me, writing is always caught up with discovery. Like E. M. Forster, I never know what I think till I see what I say. As I set out on a project, I do form a general idea of what I'd like to accomplish, so that I felt quite certain that *Ordinary Time* wouldn't turn out to be a natural foods cookbook or a study of venomous reptiles in the American Southwest, but I don't make many firm plans for carrying out my aims, since I know from experience that I'll only scrap them and devise new ones as I go along.

One point I felt certain about at the outset, however, was that I would not write a scholarly book, for which I lack both the academic preparation and the temperament. I wanted to find out how an average practitioner of Roman Catholicism goes about her daily life, what stories she tells herself about the events that befall her, how she interprets these artifacts in the light of faith, and whether such a heuristic enables her to respond meaningfully and usefully to the world around her. In other words, the book would be as purely practical as I could make it.

Nevertheless, my working style exposes me to a wealth of outside information. Once I get to my studio, I generally spend an hour or two reading serious material before sitting in front of the computer, more or less productively, for three or four hours. The reading provides an indispensable break from household life and permits me to sink from the relentlessly social hubbub raised by telephones and doorbells, not to mention the house's inmates, human and otherwise, into the silence of printed language where the writer functions. While composing and revising *Ordinary Time*, I devoted much of my reading to works at least tangentially related to religion.

On occasion, when the subject of my reading coincided with or complemented the one I was writing about, I have quoted directly from or referred to the source. Intending to take full responsibility for my reflections, however, I did not systematically take notes. Nevertheless, in subtle ways I'm sure that much of my reading shaped my thinking, and I want to acknowledge my indebtedness. The following list contains most of the works I've read or reread (or misread) in whole or in part while working on *Ordinary Time*.

Allott, Philip. *Eunomia: New Order for a New World*. New York: Oxford University Press, 1990.

Bachelard, Gaston. *The Poetics of Reverie*. Boston: Beacon Press, 1960.

Bloom, Harold, and David Rosenberg. *The Book of J*. New York: Grove Weidenfeld, 1990.

Boff, Leonardo. *Faith on the Edge: Religion and Marginalized Existence*. San Francisco: Harper & Row, 1989.

Bokenkotter, Thomas. *A Concise History of the Catholic Church*, rev. ed. Garden City, N.Y.: Doubleday, 1979.

The Book of Common Prayer. New York: The Church Pension Fund, 1945.

Brown, Peter. *The Body and Society: Men, Women, and Sexual Renunciation in Early Christianity*. New York: Columbia University Press, 1988.

Butler's Lives of the Saints, ed. Michael Walsh. San Francisco: HarperCollins, 1991.

Bynum, Caroline Walker, Stevan Harrell, and Paula Richman. *Gender and Religion: On the Complexity of Symbols*. Boston: Beacon Press, 1986.

Carmody, Denise Lardner. *The Double Cross: Ordination, Abortion, and Catholic Feminism*. New York: Crossroad, 1986.

Christ, Carol P., and Judith Plaskow, eds. *Womanspirit Rising: A Feminist Reader in Religion*. San Francisco: Harper & Row, 1979.

The Code of Canon Law in English translation, prepared by The Canon Law Society of Great Britain and Ireland. London: Collins, 1983.

Daly, Mary. *Beyond God the Father: Toward a Philosophy of Women's Liberation*. Boston: Beacon Press, 1973.

―――. *The Church and the Second Sex*. Boston: Beacon Press, 1968.

Devine, George. *A Case for Roman Catholicism*. Morristown, N.J.: Silver Burdett, 1975.

Fox, Matthew. *Creation Spirituality: Liberating Gifts for the Peoples of the Earth*. San Francisco: Harper, 1991.

————. *Original Blessing: A Primer in Creation Spirituality.* Santa Fe, N.M.: Bear & Company, 1983.

Goldenberg, Naomi R. *Changing of the Gods: Feminism and the End of Traditional Religions.* Boston: Beacon Press, 1979.

John Paul II. *On the Dignity and Vocation of Women.* Apostolic Letter, 1988.

Julian of Norwich. *Revelations of Divine Love,* trans. Clifton Walters. London: Penguin, 1966.

Kung, Hans, Josef van Ess, Heinrich von Stietencron, and Heinz Bechert. *Christianity and the World Religions: Paths to Dialogue with Islam, Hinduism, and Buddhism.* Garden City, N.Y.: Doubleday, 1986.

Lieblich, Julia. *Sisters: Lives of Devotion and Defiance.* New York: Ballantine Books, 1992.

Lupton, Robert D. *Theirs Is the Kingdom: Celebrating the Gospel in Urban America,* ed. Barbara R. Thompson. San Francisco: Harper & Row, 1989.

Martin, Emily. *The Woman in the Body: A Cultural Analysis of Reproduction.* Boston: Beacon Press, 1987.

Mason, Mary G. "The Other Voice: Autobiographies of Women Writers." In *Autobiography: Essays Theoretical and Critical,* ed. James Olney. Princeton, N.J.: Princeton University Press, 1980.

Meister Eckhart. *The Essential Sermons, Commentaries, Treatises, and Defense,* trans. Edmund Colledge and Bernard McGinn. New York: Paulist Press, 1981.

Morrow, Louis LaRavoire. *My Catholic Faith: A Manual of Religion.* Kenosha, Wisc.: My Mission House, 1949.

The New Oxford Annotated Bible with the Apocrypha, eds. Herbert G. May and Bruce M. Metzger. New York: Oxford University Press, 1973.

Plaskow, Judith, and Carol P. Christ, eds. *Weaving the Visions: New Patterns in Feminist Spirituality.* San Francisco: Harper & Row, 1989.

Ranke-Heinemann, Uta. *Eunuchs for the Kingdom of Heaven: Women, Sexuality, and the Catholic Church,* trans. Peter Heinegg. New York: Doubleday, 1990.

Ricoeur, Paul. *The Symbolism of Evil,* trans. Emerson Buchanan. Boston: Beacon Press, 1967.

Roberts, David E. *Existentialism and Religious Belief.* New York: Oxford University Press, 1969.

Ruether, Rosemary Radford. *Disputed Questions: On Being a Christian.* Maryknoll, N.Y.: Orbis, 1989.

———. *The Radical Kingdom: The Western Experience of Messianic Hope.* New York: Paulist Press, 1970.

———. *Sexism and God-Talk: Toward a Feminist Theology.* Boston: Beacon, 1983.

———. *Women-Church: Theology and Practice of Feminist Liturgical Communities.* San Francisco: Harper & Row, 1986.

Sawicki, Jana. *Disciplining Foucault: Feminism, Power, and the Body.* New York: Routledge, 1991.

Schüssler Fiorenza, Elisabeth. *Bread Not Stone: The Challenge of Feminist Biblical Interpretation.* Boston: Beacon Press, 1984.

———. *In Memory of Her.* N.Y.: Crossroad, 1984.